Religion

Reality Behind the Myths

Jonas Atlas

IFF
BOOKS

Winchester, UK
Washington, USA

JOHN HUNT PUBLISHING

First published by iff Books, 2023
iff Books is an imprint of John Hunt Publishing Ltd., No. 3 East Street, Alresford,
Hampshire SO24 9EE, UK
office@jhpbooks.com
www.johnhuntpublishing.com
www.iff-books.com

For distributor details and how to order please visit the 'Ordering' section on our website.

Text copyright: Jonas Atlas 2022

ISBN: 978 1 80341 182 8
978 1 80341 183 5 (ebook)
Library of Congress Control Number: 2022934408

A CIP catalogue record for this book is available from the British Library.

Originally published in Dutch as Religie Herzien: Voorbij het wij-zij-denken van
seculier versus religieus, Standaard Uitgeverij, 2020

Design: Matthew Greenfield

Primary editing by Andrea Reeve

UK: Printed and bound by CPI Group (UK) Ltd, Croydon, CR0 4YY
Printed in North America by CPI GPS partners

We operate a distinctive and ethical publishing philosophy in
all areas of our business, from our global network of authors to
production and worldwide distribution.

Contents

Previous books by the same author

Jonas Atlas, *Re-visioning Sufism*
Yunus Publishing, 2019, 978-9492689030

Jonas Atlas, *Halal Monk: A Christian on a Journey through Islam*
Yunus Publishing, 2015, 978-9081499644

Jonas Atlas, Breath: *The inner essence of meditation and prayer*
Yunus Publishing, 2014, 978-9081499613

Introduction

Despite "religion" being a core theme of many contemporary debates, a solid and settled definition of the concept has not yet been reached. Several possibilities have been proposed by academics, yet they vary greatly, and no single definition has become widely accepted. As such, it is not easy to clearly determine what exactly we are talking about when we discuss "all that religious stuff."

However, the absence of such an agreed upon definition does not seem to stop us from frequently talking about it. With or without a clear definition, we mostly assume we are able to recognize religious phenomena when we see them. After all, we have the feeling "that religious stuff" has some specific and common characteristics. Those characteristics can be summarized in seven basic assumptions about religion:

1. *Religions are determined by a series of dogmatic beliefs and well-defined rules of conduct that adherents must follow.* This is probably the most central aspect of what makes religion so religious.

2. *Religions are structured hierarchically* and those who occupy top positions within the power structure determine both the content of the faith and the rules delineating the appropriate behavior of the followers.

3. *Religions can be clearly distinguished, based on their beliefs, rules, and structures.* Which means, for example, that we can easily separate Christianity from Buddhism or straightforwardly differentiate Muslims from Hindus.

4. *Spirituality and mysticism contrast with religion.* Spirituality is perceived as beautiful and liberating, while religion is seen as limiting. This results in a large group of people stating they are spiritual, but not religious.

5. *Science and religion are at odds with each other.* After all, religion is based on faith. Science, on the other hand, is based on facts and reason.

6. *Religions are dangerous because their irrational truth claims inevitably provoke violence.* This immediately leads to the final assumption.

7. *A secular society is completely different (and inherently better) than a religious society.*

Every day, we find variations of these assumptions in all kinds of newspaper articles, political debates, and TV documentaries. In modern societies, in which people consider themselves to be secular, they constitute a basic view of religion.

The only problem is that none of these assumptions are true. Instead of reasoned ideas, they are unfounded assumptions. Instead of facts, they are modern myths, and just like the myths of other times, they are a staple of everyone's education— not because they offer us a better insight into the world, but because they provide a persuasive symbolism for describing what is "good" and "evil." These assumptions therefore do not provide a greater knowledge of our society, but they do provide a kind of emotional-existential lens through which we interpret society. They ensure an "us versus them" mentality of secular versus religious.

For many people, however, these seven assumptions are accepted elements of a clear conceptual framework. They are not considered to be fabrications at all. Rather, they are seen as an undeniable reality because, in past centuries, fact and fiction have become strongly intertwined. The divide between secularism and religiosity developed into a self-evident foundation of the dominant worldview.

With this book then, I would like to make a counter argument. I want to unravel fact and fiction. I want to put the subject of "religion" in a new perspective by questioning the basic premises on which the current view is built. I want to clarify why these seven commonplace assumptions about religion indeed do not describe reality but function as myths instead.

The structure of this book is simple: in each chapter I take a closer look at one of these seven basic assumptions by extensively investigating, questioning and/or disproving various elements of the assumptions. However, I will not limit myself to deconstruction. At the end of each chapter, I suggest how we might approach its theme from a different perspective and, as a result, develop a new vision of religion.

This approach structures all chapters but one because, after discussing the first three myths, an interlude seemed necessary to explain why we are continually confronted with the difficulty of defining religion. This interlude also briefly outlines the fascinating history behind the word "religion" and points out some important and often overlooked sociopolitical aspects of that history.

To make the whole book as accessible as possible, I have used a lot of concrete examples. These examples, more than philosophical and theoretical considerations, clearly show why the current frameworks about religion so frequently fall short. Taken as a whole, they cease to be apparent exceptions to the rule and instead become strong challenges *to* the rule.

Nevertheless, this book in no way contradicts the findings of current religious studies. Most of the concepts every chapter discusses are not controversial among the scholars who research that particular subject. For example, one can easily come across well-substantiated books about the intimate relationship between faith and science, or find academic articles about the fluid boundaries between religious traditions. Yet, generally speaking, those books and articles are limited to just one specific topic. As such, there is a lot of material available in which researchers analyze and debunk one particular assumption about religion, but, to my knowledge, those materials have not been compiled in an organized manner before. One of the main purposes of this book is therefore to uncover the common threads that connect the various public debates which concern religion.

However, the fact that I deliberately wanted to maintain such a broad perspective was at odds with my intention to make the book concise. Therefore, in order for it to be useful for a wide audience, I was forced to impose some restrictions on my endeavor.

The first of these limitations was the choice to draw most examples from only three religious contexts: Christian, Islamic and Hindu traditions. Elements from other religious contexts are also discussed here and there, but the most elaborate examples are always connected to these three matrices of traditions. The underlying reason is simple: in recent years, both personally and professionally, I have mainly delved deeper into different branches of those religions, so, I feel most "at home" in them. On top of it, even though this brings along a certain restriction, in various sociological and theological respects they are more than distinct enough to ensure sufficient religious variety among the examples.

A second limitation lies in the choice to mostly present examples that are not too far off the spectrum of common knowledge about religion. By sticking to better known elements, less elaborate explanations are needed. It also immediately ensured I could reduce the references to a minimum. When the information I provide can be found in an average handbook or is so uncontroversial that it is correctly described on public online encyclopedias, I omitted references. Those who are not familiar with certain examples and want to confirm their veracity can easily look them up on the Internet. As such, I only give further sources and references when it comes to issues that are more specialized or somewhat more disputed. (That being said, it is worth noting that by "common examples" I mean aspects of religious history and theology that are relatively well known within the field of religious studies. Most of them will probably make many readers raise their eyebrows, because even when they are not controversial, they are often completely ignored in mainstream narratives about religion.)

Finally, I chose to limit myself to the core essence of my argument. I therefore tried not to weigh the book down with related tangents. That is why extra quotations, supporting examples, references to the work of leading religious scholars and comments which are linked to more specialized debates were included as endnotes only. In addition, I have placed a few short text boxes with relevant facts throughout the chapters. Readers can thus choose whether or not they would like to engage with these short elaborations on particular topics.

But what are commandments worth if one cannot occasionally sin against them? As such, I do not follow the guidelines just outlined on all pages of the book. Here and there I do go deeper into some religious phenomena that are less well known, and which need some more extensive explanation. However, there is a specific reason why I chose to include these more drawn-out anecdotes after all: they will probably put a smile on the reader's face. That is of great importance to me because I believe investigative analysis and fun should go hand in hand more often — especially when it comes to religion.

Myth #1

Religions Are Determined by a Series of Dogmatic Beliefs and Well-defined Rules of Conduct That Adherents Must Follow

Why a belief in one or more gods is not the basis of religion

Religion is primarily concerned with a belief in God. That is the commonplace assumption.

Most certainly, such a belief is a core element of the two religious traditions with the largest number of adherents: Christianity and Islam. Together, their followers comprise more than half of the world's population, and it is difficult to deny that their theologies, rituals, and ethics largely focus on a transcendent creator God who ensures both mercy and justice in the world.

Religious demographics

In 2010, the Pew Research Center estimated the number of Christians at 32 percent of the world's population and the number of Muslims at 24 percent. The third largest group (16 percent) was identified by the survey as "unaffiliated" (that is to say, people who explicitly do not consider themselves to be part of any particular religious tradition). The fourth group were Hindus (15 percent) and the fifth Buddhists (7 percent). What sometimes surprises people about these figures is the relatively low percentage of Jews in the world, as they make up only 0.2 percent of the world's population.[1]

Of course, religions do not always worship just one God. Some traditions are polytheistic or encompass a belief in a whole variety of supernatural beings. An obvious example thereof would be the pantheon of the ancient Greeks. In it, gods and goddesses such as Zeus, Aphrodite, and Athena interacted with all kinds of creatures such as titans, satyrs, and nymphs. A more contemporary example can be found in the traditions of Hinduism where we find colorful images of the god Shiva, who dances in order to balance the cosmos; of the many-armed goddess Durga, who devours all evil; and of Ganesha, who has the head of an elephant.

In the latter case, many Hindus would argue that they are actually worshipping a divine, cosmic essence when they are burning incense in front of the statues in their temples or homes. The multitude of gods are merely symbolic because behind their multiplicity lies the One Ultimate Reality, which is called Brahman. From this perspective, the various gods are but (partial) manifestations of that Brahman. For example, they might express elements of its creative energy, its destructive power, its deep beauty, or its elusiveness. Moreover, *everything* in existence is ultimately a manifestation of the One Ultimate Reality permeating all that is at every moment. As such, a large part of the Hindu traditions can, in a sense, be described as monotheistic.[2] Although, of course, Brahman is a much more "impersonal" God than the one referred to in Christian or Islamic contexts. After all, this perception of the divine is less about a God directly relating to humans, and more about a sacred essence that is present in the depth of every creature.

Such conceptualizations of the divine can be found in many other places. For example, in Taoism, the Tao is a central notion. Literally translatable as "The Way," it refers to a kind of divine dynamic that pushes everything that is in a certain direction. The Tao brings harmony between the many opposites of yin and yang: light and dark, heat and cold, creation and destruction, unity and multiplicity, and so on. According to Taoists, we should thus try to live in accordance with this underlying Tao dynamic as much as possible; for when we do so, we will achieve a better balance, both in our personal lives and in society as a whole.

Many other religious traditions can be mentioned in which "the belief in God" does not imply a belief in a supernatural figure who created the world and subsequently acts as its guardian, but these examples sufficiently clarify that the God one person believes in does not always correspond to the God another person worships. The different religions do not always uphold similar visions of the divine. One could therefore wonder whether the word "God" always carries the same meaning and, as a result, whether we can truly claim that a belief in God(s) is always at the center of every religion.

To get around this problem in trying to articulate the essence of religion, a different approach is sometimes proposed: perhaps not every religious tradition revolves around "God," but all of them at least include the belief in "transcendence." The exact interpretation of this transcendence might perhaps differ, but the common denominator would therefore be that there is "something" beyond the world and nature. Unfortunately, such an approach equally fails in providing a universal thread among the various religions.

Why the belief in "something transcendent" does not form the basis of religion either

Even though it strongly contradicts the prevailing view, it is simply not true that all religious traditions are, by definition, based on transcendent concepts. Let us return to the concept of Tao for a first example. Yes, a Taoist may consider the Tao to be an expression of a transcendent and divine power—in fact, many do—but other interpretations are equally possible. The Tao can also be considered as an inherent governing principle of the universe. From this perspective, "The Way" and the balancing patterns which can be discerned therein (the natural transition from yin to yang and vice versa) are simply facts. In this case, it ceases to be a transcendent concept and instead refers to constant processes within the cosmos. It becomes a kind of overarching natural law that is just as "non-transcendent" as gravity.

We can even go one step further and include explicitly atheistic religious groups. This may sound paradoxical, but the phenomenon does exist. Jewish atheists are a good illustration. They do not believe in God, but they do explicitly identify themselves as adherents of Judaism, regularly visit a synagogue and maintain the various traditional rituals. The movement of Humanist Judaism is an organized expression of this phenomenon, but there are atheistic Jews from many different denominations. In the United States, for example, a large-scale survey from 2018 found that this label can be applied to about ten percent of American Jews.[3]

For yet another example we can of course turn toward Buddhism. This is probably the best-known example of an ostensibly atheistic (or at least agnostic) religion. According to the oldest sources, the Buddha seemed to have little concern for "God" or "the divine." Not that he explicitly described himself as an atheist or that he outright rejected the existence of divine beings. He simply did not accord them much relevance. As far as historical sources can reconstruct the doctrine he preached, it did not seem to involve a concept of some God who rules over all of creation. When references are made to gods in some of the oldest texts that contain the Buddha's teachings, they are beings who, like humans, are subject to the universal dynamics of eternal change. As such, they too will come and go. Many Buddhist teachers of the first centuries after the Buddha therefore explicitly rejected the idea of an eternal and omnipotent God.

After all, the Buddha was primarily looking for a practical, psychological, and existential way out of suffering. To a large extent, this Buddhist endeavor comes down to accepting the fundamental transience of existence and letting go of one's attachments to anything that is bound to eventually disappear. Whoever succeeds in doing so, and thus becomes enlightened by realizing that people stumble from one illusion to another as long as they are absorbed by desires, attains nirvana. According to some scholars of religious studies, nirvana is a transcendent concept in the sense that it can be viewed as a kind of Ultimate Reality that lurks beneath all the change of the universe. That certainly is one possible interpretation. However, nirvana, which literally means "being blown out" or "being extinguished," is above all a concept by which the Buddhist tradition indicates "emptiness." It is primarily about a state of consciousness in which suffering no longer has a hold on oneself. Hence, nirvana does not necessarily have to be interpreted as something transcendent at all. Many Buddhists would not label it as such either.

Consequently, there is a long-standing debate about the question of whether Buddhism is a religion or not. Some prefer to stick to a more general term such as "philosophy" or "lifestyle." However, such a view is difficult to reconcile with the day-to-day reality of various Asian countries. In Buddhist temples in Thailand, for example, one can regularly find many Hindu gods, such as Shiva, Indra, Vishnu, and the elephant god Ganesh; Tibetan Buddhism is full of images of gods and demons, many of which are also related to the Hindu pantheon; and the traditional stories surrounding the Buddha's birth are full of paranormal events. In fact, the latter even describe how his mother became pregnant without the involvement of a man. The Buddha also took seven steps immediately after his birth and blooming lotus flowers appeared where he placed his feet.

Additionally, the daily ritual practice of many Buddhists does not revolve around some type of solitary meditation. In fact, in several countries in which Buddhism is the dominant religion, the laity does not meditate at all. Rather, they try to build up good karma by, for example, giving gifts to the mendicant monks, or living a morally correct life.[4] Also worth noting, is that whoever witnesses the prayer of those monks in their monasteries or temples—even if they belong to the most non-theistic branches of Buddhism—will not be able to ignore the strong religious atmosphere as the monks perform standardized rituals, or spend hours monotonously reciting ancient texts.

No matter how fascinating this discussion might be, the point here is not to propose a final answer. Of importance here is merely the discussion itself since it presents us with an explicit illustration of the multifaceted way in which some traditions deal with the divine. Even if some would argue that there are non-religious forms of Buddhism, taken as a whole, this broad tradition undoubtedly contains all kinds of religious elements.

It should therefore be clear: religions are not necessarily determined by belief in one or more gods. On top of it, when we do encounter conceptualizations of the divine in different religions, these can encompass varying (and not always comparable) perceptions of divine manifestation. Likewise, the proposal that religions, in essence, always focus on "something transcendent" does not resolve the lack of common denominator. No matter how general or abstract the concept we accept, in the end, we will not be able to pinpoint specific elements that apply to all religions universally.[5]

Even *within each individual religion,* belief and faith are not the defining or binding factor. Religious traditions can rarely be defined by a set of specific convictions since adherents of the same religion can have very different interpretations of crucial elements within their tradition. The last example of the Buddhist variations in ritual worship of gods already hinted at this. However, it can be helpful to delve somewhat deeper into this matter.

On the variations of beliefs *within* religions

I opened this chapter referring to the belief in a personal God within Christianity and Islam. I contrasted this belief with the Hindu view of an impersonal God to indicate how varied "beliefs in God" can be. In reality, however, different approaches toward the divine cannot be neatly divided among religions. If the monotheistic approaches of Christians or Muslims are examined in more depth, one regularly encounters descriptions of God that are miles away from any anthropomorphic interpretation. Many of them see God primarily as a profound spiritual force that created the cosmos, sustains life, pervades everything, and resonates within their lives. They have no affinity at all with the stereotypical bearded man who closely observes all people from behind the clouds. Instead, they interpret Biblical or Qur'anic expressions about God who "speaks," "looks," or "acts" as purely metaphorical expressions that are only described this way as a means to invoke a complex divinity which is infinitely beyond all imagination and thus beyond words.

The variation of images of God among Christians and Muslims

The supposition that many Christians and Muslims have a rather "impersonal" image of God is, first of all, based on personal experiences and conversations. However, for those who do not find this a compelling argument, I can also refer to one of the few large-scale studies on variations of approaches to the divine, conducted by the Pew Research Center in 2018. The study examined what Americans exactly mean when they say they believe in God. Among American Christians, 18 percent say they do not believe in "the Biblical God," while they do believe in "a higher power or spiritual force in the universe." Among Jews, that percentage rises to 56 percent. Moreover, when we have a further look at the meaning people assign to the terms "a Biblical God" or "a higher power," it appears that both groups mainly agree on the idea that God loves people and protects them. Major differences only become apparent when the question is asked whether God also determines what happens in their personal lives. Of those who say they believe in a Biblical God, 70 percent answer in the affirmative, compared to 25 percent of the group who believe in a higher spiritual power. But when asked whether God actually talks to them, the percentages drop to just 40 percent for those who believe in the Biblical God, and to 16 percent for those believing in a higher spiritual power.[6]

It is of course important to note that the situation in the United States is not representative of the situation in other countries. For example, in the Netherlands and Belgium, the two countries in which I spend most of my time, the percentages of Christians who do not identify with a "Biblical God" but rather see God as "a higher power or spiritual force in the universe" is likely to be much higher. Research in those countries revealed that only 17 percent of Christians believe in a personal God, and less than half hold that Jesus is the Son of God or was sent by God. The percentages are slightly higher among Dutch Protestants. However, even within this group 33 percent do not believe in the divine character of Christ.[7]

It is also important to remember that impersonal perceptions of God in traditions with a strong theistic focus are not limited to "modern" conceptions of God. Many classical texts of great theologians become completely incomprehensible when read through the lens of a God who is a concrete, definable, supernatural being. When such texts try to describe an omnipresent God, who penetrates every aspect of existence to its very core, they seem to invoke a concept such as "The One Ultimate Reality." That is why the great Islamic sage Mevlana

Rumi was fond of referring to the Qur'anic verses that describe God as being "closer to you than your jugular vein"[8] and that declare: "wherever you turn, there is His Face."[9] The words of the Christian Meister Eckhart sound very similar when he states that "whoever possesses God in their being, has Him in a divine manner, and He shines out to them in all things; for them all things taste of God and in all things it is God's image that they see. God is always radiant in them; they are inwardly detached from the world and are in-formed by the loving presence of their God."[10] Such statements are only comprehensible if one does not see God merely as a distinct, transcendent supreme being, but also experiences Him as a deeply immanent reality.

Conversely, I will qualify my earlier description of Hinduism. For not all Hindus approach the many gods as manifestations of the One Ultimate Reality (Brahman) or as metaphorical figures. Some believe in the reified existence of multiple gods and thus consider them to be real beings in themselves. We can also refer to the existence of the Bhakti movement. This is a strand of Hinduism in which devotees focus their own spiritual devotion on one specific god from the Hindu pantheon. In fact, since Bhaktis see that particular God as *the* manifestation of Brahman, their way of relating to the divine is, in some respects, similar to the concept of incarnation in Christianity. So, in this case, we might indeed speak of a "personal God" — or at least a personal relationship with that God.

Similar variations can easily be noticed in many other elements of faith such as expectations of life after death. To give one striking example: a considerable proportion of Christians do not believe the afterlife continues in a separate dimension of existence (let alone in a form of "heaven" or "hell"). Moreover, a survey in the United States shows that 29 percent of American

Christians believe in reincarnation. Among American Catholics, that figure increases to 36 percent.[11] In contrast, for a branch of Hinduism that *does not* believe in reincarnation, we can refer to the materialist and atheist Charvaka movement.

Besides the fact that there can be enormous variations within a faith, even with respect to some core elements, it is also significant that "being convinced of something" is often not the most important issue in the adherence to a particular tradition. The way of life and the ensuing practices often bear much greater significance.

As I already mentioned, there are quite a few people who strongly identify as Jewish and follow many Jewish customs, but do not believe in God. The five pillars of Islam are another good example of conduct and behavior being sometimes more significant than solemn truth claims. Generally, these five pillars are considered the core elements of Islam, yet only one of them pertains directly to faith. The other four pillars are all common religious practices: fasting, praying, giving alms, and making a pilgrimage. The sole "pillar of faith" expresses two simple assertions: "There is no God but *the* God and Muhammad is one of his messengers." In order to convert to Islam, it suffices to subscribe to these tenets.

In this regard, the difference between orthodoxy and orthopraxy comes to the fore: orthodoxy concerns religious traditions that emphasize a correct *teaching* (the Greek "ortho" means "straight" and "doxo" means "conviction"), while orthopraxy concerns religious traditions which revolve around correct *practice* (the Greek "praxis" means "doing"). The various religions cannot always be neatly categorized along these lines, but the terms do clarify why we should not assume that every religious tradition trends toward the side of orthodoxy. Many traditions have a stronger emphasis on orthopraxy since, for a lot of people, performing rituals from their tradition or following a certain way of life is a lot more important than their convictions or inner certitudes.

Yet, let us not exaggerate the adherence to orthopraxy either. After all, there are exceptions to every rule.

On the variety of rules and regulations within religions

When taking a broad perspective of any religion, one can easily observe quite a bit of flexibility in how the prescriptions are perceived and practiced. By way of illustration, we can return to the five pillars of Islam. Not all Muslims pray five times a day; the pilgrimage to Mecca only needs to be carried out if one has the financial means to do so; and the exact interpretation of the zakat (alms to the poor) differs greatly from country to country.

Another example, which deserves some elaboration, is the place of alcohol within Islam. Theoretically speaking, alcohol is prohibited among Muslims. Yet, in a dominantly Muslim country such as Turkey, beer, wine and raki are commonly produced. Anyone who walks through the shopping streets of big cities such as Istanbul or Ankara knows that alcohol is a ubiquitous element of social life. Yet Turks are no less Muslim because of it—and certainly no less "religious." Moreover, they do not differ that much from the many Islamic politicians, poets, and mystics, who, over the centuries, held wine in high esteem. For example, the ninth century CE saw a cultural and religious flourishing under the reign of Harun al-Rashid. Life in the palace of this Abbasid caliph also served as the setting for several stories in the famous collection *One Thousand and One Nights*. Nonetheless, in that same palace people regularly sang, danced, and drank. The same was true in the sixteenth-century courts of Babur, the founder of the Indian Mughal dynasty, and of Shah Ismail, the founder of the Persian Safavid Empire.[12]

Then there is also the famous fourteenth-century poet Hafez who is held in very high esteem to this day. Every day, buses packed with schoolchildren are driven to his grave to recite his poems reverentially. Yet, these poems contain several references to drunkenness, as in these verses:

Don't talk to me of sugar, or of any food that's sweet;
Sweetness for me is on your lips when your and my lips meet.
I'll haunt these ruins while within the ruins of my heart
The treasure of my love for you is lodged and won't depart.
Why do you talk to me of shame—shame has become my
name—
Or reputation, when my reputation is my shame?
We drink our wine, we flirt, and we're licentious—yes, but
who
Is in this city where we live of whom this isn't true?
And don't go to the morals officer to make a fuss—
He's on the constant lookout too for pleasure, just like us.
This is no time to sit, Hafez, without your wine and lover;
Jasmine's and roses' days are here, and Ramadan is over.[13]

It is generally held that Hafez meant such verses merely metaphorically, describing the mystical experience of being intoxicated by profound union with the divine. However, even if he predominantly had this deeper layer of meaning in mind, we can at least notice how lavishly he used the metaphor. This should not come as a surprise since he moved within the elite circles of his time, where wine flowed freely. So, at the very least, his listeners were likely to appreciate such a metaphor because of their more literal personal experiences.

As a result, anyone who wants to argue that every Muslim who drinks alcohol is not a "real" Muslim is faced with a paradox since such a view implies that important Islamic figures, who were respected for centuries, suddenly cease to be "real" examples of the way in which Islam was experienced in the past. On the other hand, anyone who claims that they too were Muslims must conclude that "the adherence to religious rules and regulations" is a very relative concept—even within a religious tradition that shows a strong propensity for orthopraxy in some respects.

This certainly does not only apply to Islam. In every religious tradition there is an enormous variety of customs and lifestyles. Let me give one last example from Christianity. Many Western Europeans are convinced that all of their Christian ancestors regularly and devoutly attended church. Yet this assumption is not borne out by fact. When we have a look at historiography that finds itself a bit outside the mainstream, we can find information which contradicts the commonplace image. For example, a different picture emerges from Emma Wilby's renowned book on folk beliefs and witchcraft in early modern England:

> In our own century, novelists and filmmakers unconsciously perpetuate the notion of the idyllic Christian community of Britain past: every member of the parish, from the poorest cottar in his homespun jerkin to the lord of the manor in his velvets and ruff, all coming together to worship in a candle-lit church—the gulf in rank and earthly fortunes which normally separated them being momentarily bridged by the metaphysical certainties and emotional comforts of established belief. But the reality was rather different. In many parts of England and Scotland churches were without a resident priest. (...) A significant proportion of common folk seldom attended church at all. Contemporaries complained that it was quite common for only half of the parish to be present at Sunday worship and in 1635 one pamphleteer lamented that it "really was a case of two or three persons gathered in God's name." (...) Of those who attended church, many just went through the motions with little real understanding. A large proportion of the laity could not recite the Lord's Prayer or Ten Commandments and knew little of Christian scripture or doctrine, one observer complaining in 1606 that people "knew more about Robin Hood than they did about the stories in the Bible."[14]

It may not be congruent with our current image, but among sixteenth- and seventeenth-century rural communities in England and Scotland, Christianity was not all that life-encompassing. According to Wilby, people were largely concerned with something completely different: "The guiding principles in the lives of many ordinary people in early modern Britain were essentially 'animist' rather than Christian."[15]

This suggests that the beliefs of the average British layperson at the time concerned supernatural beings such as elves, fairies, and goblins just as much as Christian teachings. To illustrate, it was a daily ritual for many housewives to leave bread and water in the kitchen at night for the fairies, in hopes that the fairies would leave some silver in their shoes—an obvious precursor to the customs surrounding Saint Nicholas Day or Christmas, when children place a shoe or a sock at the chimney hoping that it will be filled with candy or presents.

Some figures who were known to be in close contact with supernatural beings, were sought out by people who were sick, who had lost an important item, or who thought someone might have stolen from them. In general, these figures were women. Today we would talk about witches, but at the time, they used other terms such as "cunning women." The word "cunning" in this case does not carry the connotation of "sly" or "shrewd," but rather of "knowledgeable" and "skilled." Thus, it implied wise women who had privileged access to this other realm. The word "witch" also invokes an image of an old lady living all alone in a small house in the woods where she brews potent drinks with freshly picked herbs, but the cunning women had many customers and consequently had a recognized status in public society—although some had better reputations and become more famous than others.[16]

In her book, Wilby takes an in-depth look at the life story of Bessie Dunlop, a sixteenth-century cunning woman. Bessie testified that she was in close contact with a spirit who told her how to heal people. After revealing himself to her several times, he asked her if she would renounce her Christian faith in exchange for wealth, which he might procure for her. Such a question often came up as part of a pact the spirit wished to establish with the cunning woman. However, Bessie was resolute: "No, I would never do such a thing, even if I was dragged at a horse's tail."[17]

This naturally confronts us with an interesting phenomenon. Someone like Bessie Dunlop did not always go to church devoutly. In her daily life she was more concerned with practices that some would consider very "unchristian" today. Nevertheless, it was clear *to her* that she was a Christian and she would never give up on her faith. She was certainly no exception in this regard. In the lives of many of her contemporaries (if not most), animism and magic went hand in hand with their Christian beliefs and rituals. They simply did not perceive any discrepancy between the two.

These examples are, of course, at odds with the widespread idea that individuals who adhere to a religion always toe the line. It is generally assumed that discarding religious rules and regulations only became possible in modern times. However, anyone who delves deeper into the historical realities of religious life can easily see that all religions have always shown some level of "unlawful" behavior.

Incidentally, this does not only apply to the flexibility of religious rules. It also applies to explicit *criticism of* those rules, which is also not a "modern" phenomenon. It is as common to religious traditions as the rules themselves.

How criticizing dogmatic thinking is part and parcel of the history of all religious traditions

Most certainly, rituals and practices are a prominent part of the everyday faith of most major religions today and a religious elite often tries to determine the contours of these rituals and practices. However, this does not mean that the ruling power or its prescriptions are never questioned. On the contrary, in every tradition it is easy to find texts containing the teachings of preachers, poets, mystics, and spiritual teachers who openly critique strict legalism and power abuse. Moreover, such a critical attitude is often present in the statements of various figures who are considered to be founders or central figures of a religion. For example, Jesus made some piercing remarks about the hypocrisy of the scribes and the Pharisees:

> They are seated in the chair of Moses. Therefore, do whatever they tell you, and observe it. But don't do what they do, because they don't practice what they teach. They tie up heavy loads that are hard to carry and put them on people's shoulders, but they themselves aren't willing to lift a finger to move them.[18]

In order to support his point, Jesus sometimes referred to the authority of the Torah: "Go and learn what this means: 'I desire mercy and not sacrifice.'"[19]

In a completely different tradition such as Taoism, we can read the following words of Lao Tzu in the Tao Te Ching:

> A man of the highest virtue does not keep to virtue and that is why he has virtue. A man of the lowest virtue never strays from virtue and that is why he is without virtue. The former never acts yet leaves nothing undone. The latter acts but there are things left undone. A man of the highest benevolence acts, but from no ulterior motive. A man of the highest rectitude acts, but from ulterior motive. A man most conversant in the rites acts, but when no one responds, rolls up his sleeves and resorts to persuasion by force. Hence when The Way was lost there was virtue; when virtue was lost there was benevolence; when benevolence was lost there

was rectitude; when rectitude was lost there were the rites. The rites are the wearing thin of loyalty and good faith and the beginning of disorder. (...) Therefore, the full-grown man sets his heart upon the substance rather than the husk; upon the fruit rather than the flower. Truly, he prefers what is within to what is without.[20]

In addition to such words from the forebears which were written down in foundational texts, we can find thousands of other examples of historical figures who are thought of as pinnacles of their faith's values, yet who engaged flexibly with the rules of their religion. The message is often the same: rules and rituals mean absolutely nothing if they do not have spiritual sincerity. And vice versa: if they do have spiritual sincerity, it makes little difference whether the details are adhered to. Small acts and everyday prayers can have tremendous value if they are performed with deep dedication, while grandiose rituals can be eroded if performed with the intent to show off one's piety.

Throughout the history of every tradition, we therefore encounter different trends. On the one hand, certain figures and groups insist that specific rules of conduct and ritual practices must be strictly followed by everyone. Some even try to regulate their entire life on (their particular interpretation of) certain scriptural verses and/or sayings of important historic figures. This tendency is often initiated or demonstrated by figures who obtained positions of social, political or religious power (and frequently all three of them). We can for example see such inclinations in Islamic Wahhabism, Christian Puritanism, or the Hindu nationalist Rashtriya Swayamsevak Sangh.

On the other hand, one can also encounter individuals and communities who wish to discard excessive regulation and inordinate legalism. They generally argue for an internalized spirituality and/or a social engagement that keeps itself as far away as possible from any formalized regulatory system. Such persuasions often arise as explicit forms of opposition, in response to existing power structures. Some examples are Christian liberation theology, the Islamic Qalandariyya, and the Hindu Sant Mat movement.[21] However, it would be difficult to describe this second tendency as "less religious" than those who favor more defined regulatory systems. Those who belong to each branch of the respective tradition often base their convictions on verses from the same scriptures, and on statements attributed to the same forebears.

It goes without saying that this is only a theoretical split. In daily practice, most strands within every religious tradition occupy a middle position somewhere between these two poles.

In accordance with all of this, the behavior of believers also does not have to meticulously correspond with the contents of old scriptures. Being connected to a certain tradition does not suddenly turn people into some sort of religious robot, whose behavior is completely determined by the content of their faith's holy scriptures. Some people with highly rationalist and modernist leanings, or with a strong aversion to religion nevertheless seem convinced of just such a thing. In fact, in somewhat more moderate forms, this idea is actually quite commonplace. As such, it will be beneficial to briefly explain why it is a problematic assumption.

Why holy scriptures mainly serve as guidelines and not as strict prescriptions

Let us perhaps start with acknowledging that not every religious tradition has a few or even one foundational source. Some traditions do (or did) not rely on holy scriptures at all, such as many forms of shamanism and animism, which include modern, Neopagan forms of witchcraft and nature worship. In other traditions there is such a wide range of important texts that it is difficult to speak of one overarching sacred canon. In the Hindu traditions, for example, we can refer to a large collection of highly respected philosophical, mythological, and theological works, the majority of which are never read by the common people. Many Hindus have rarely seen the Vedas, Puranas, or Upanishads up close. As such, they certainly are not the determinant factor in their daily religious life.[22]

Subsequently, when we have a good look at the traditions for which one or a few source texts *do* play a central role, it is difficult to ignore the enormous variation in the ways these texts are dealt with. Throughout history, many scribes and theologians have engaged with these texts in different manners, and they have often done so with a healthy dose of rational thinking. For example, this can be seen in the use of a common hermeneutical principle among Islamic scholars which distinguishes between "universal" and "specific" verses of the Qur'an. Universal verses, such as those that call for compassion and justice, are always applicable to everyone. Specific verses, on the other hand, only apply in the precise historical context to which they refer. As such, specific verses must be contextualized in light of the universal in order to understand them properly. For instance, the Qur'anic verses about marriage must always be interpreted with the more general verses about love and fidelity as background.[23]

Text-oriented traditions frequently also have quite a bit of room for differing interpretations as well. One illustration of this is the fact that authorities of the Christian church never decreed that biblical stories should be taken literally. In the past, people did turn to the Bible as a source of historical information, but whenever new discoveries contradicted the texts, it was always possible to fall back on a symbolic reading without detracting from the sacrality of the text. Church fathers such as Origen in the third century and Augustine in the fifth century indicated that the stories about creation and the patriarchs could, and in many cases *should*, be read allegorically. So, contrary to common assumptions, interpreting holy books symbolically or metaphorically is not a new or "modern" phenomenon. It is actually pretty normative—in all traditions.[24]

Origen and Augustine on a metaphorical reading of the Bible

In *De principiis*, a book in which he sets out the basic principles of the Christian faith, Origen explicitly supports a metaphorical reading of the Bible. First he gives several examples of mythological stories and then he states: "I do not think anyone will doubt that these are figurative expressions which indicate certain mysteries through a semblance of history and not through actual events. (...) And the careful reader will detect thousands of other passages like this in the gospels, which will convince him that events which did not take place at all are woven into the records of what literally did happen."[25]

Augustine also was clear about this when he wrote a treatise on how to interpret Genesis. He gave a somewhat convoluted argument, but it can be summarized as follows: it is impossible that the authors of the different books of the Bible wrote things that were manifestly untrue or stupid. So, if some passages seem to go against the facts or contradict certain knowledge we have gathered in our own times, then that passage is only meant to be understood spiritually and/or metaphorically. This is why he argues vehemently against believers who use the Bible to refute established knowledge concerning nature. In his view, they undermine the credibility of Christians. If people do not believe Christians because they say ridiculous things about worldly matters, he argues, then people certainly will not take them seriously when it comes to far more important spiritual matters.[26]

Obviously, we can find plenty of people in various traditions who *do* take their sacred scriptures literally. They read each story as factual and try to apply each precept as strictly as possible. However, even they can never do so with complete consistency. Some passages are contradictory or paradoxical, requiring them to let one take precedence over the other. Likewise, it is rarely (or perhaps never) possible to abide by all the commandments—not in the least because the scriptures hail from very different times and contexts. As a result, even literalists are constantly making choices concerning which rules to follow. They too never follow the book "as it is written." They too select and interpret its contents all the time. Yet, even if we disregard such inconsistencies and even if their interpretations appear more literal to some, that still does not mean that their approach is (or should be) the norm for all "believers" of the tradition in question.

By now, it should be clear that we cannot assume religions everywhere are always determined by a series of dogmatic beliefs and well-defined rules of faith to which the believers must adhere. Although this is probably the central assumption about what makes religion so religious, it is not borne out by the facts. After all, there are no beliefs or rules that universally apply to all religions. Even within specific religions, there are seldom any dogmas or specific religious rules of conduct that every believer, by definition, adheres to.

The concept of "dogma" is ultimately a Christian (and more specifically, a Catholic) concept that does not apply to most other religions because there are few, if any, shared foundational beliefs. Also, while some would like to impose strict rules on their fellow adherents, in the complex history of the great religious traditions—and the many cultural variations that these entail—those rules prove to be extremely flexible.

The following chapters will provide many more examples,

but, for now, the ones already given should suffice, for they revealed the need to look at religion in a different way if we wish to find out what truly comprises its core.

A different look at the core elements of religious traditions

In this chapter I certainly do not wish to claim that faith never matters, or that every religious way of life is completely noncommittal. That would make no sense at all. Most certainly, religious beliefs (whether meaningful or not) and religious habits (whether problematic or not) have a significant impact on people's lives. All I hope to point out is that these two elements alone do not constitute the all-determining essence of religion, as many people seem to think. By focusing too narrowly on beliefs and commandments, we lose sight of other dimensions which are just as, if not more, important.

One of those dimensions is "experience." We can see this clearly in the testimonies of converts, for example. Many converts do not refer to specific doctrines or codes of conduct as the initial pull toward another tradition, but rather relate their conversion to an experience: an overwhelming existential experience that makes them see the world in a new light; an experience of "finally finding their place" when encountering a specific religious group; or an uplifting experience when encountering the person who eventually became their spiritual teacher.

Experiences are also of great importance to the internal development of religions. Since time immemorial, humankind has been looking for ways to express the experiences of life and death, of helplessness and hope, of suffering and inner strength. As best we can, we try to make sense of those experiences, we try to pass on the wisdom they brought us, and we often look for opportunities to relive some of them—especially when it comes to experiences of existential connection, divine closeness, or expanded consciousness.

With this in mind, religions are largely an attempt to describe an infinite array of life experiences with mythological images; to place those experiences within a cosmological perspective; to mark them with rituals; and to reinforce their meanings with spiritual practices.

This is not a new idea. It is encountered in all kinds of literature which diverges from the dominant modernist view and embraces a more positive view of religion. In various academic circles too, "experience" is used as a basic concept for analyzing religious phenomena. Many famous names of comparative religion including William James, Mircea Eliade, Rudolf Otto, Huston Smith, Jonathan Hick, Wilfred Cantwell Smith, Ninian Smart and Karen Armstrong subscribe to such a view. They see religious experiences as profound existential experiences of awe, liberation, and mystery through a confrontation with "something" that transcends us as human beings. And from this perspective, they see religions not only as the diverse cultural expressions of such experiences, but also as an amalgam of rituals and practices that offer the opportunity of partaking in these experiences.

However, the concept of "experience" does not explain all religious phenomena either. Although experience is often an important element, it is not the one binding thread of religion. Exactly because of the enormous differences between the various religious traditions (and their subdivisions), we can identify certain groups for which experience seems to be of little importance to their daily religious life. Considering the fact that, within more orthoprax communities, it is important to maintain formal traditions with precision because they have always been performed in a particular manner, it should be clear that some nuances are needed. Even if certain traditional practices were originally based on an existential experience, that does not necessarily mean that they are carried out for centuries for the sake of seeking an identical experience.

Moreover, one cannot guarantee that the same experience will always be invoked by performing the same ritual. Sometimes people just perform certain rituals for no other reason than the fact that it is their custom.

In addition to the experiential aspect of religion, another vital dimension to consider is the aesthetic one. There are many examples of this dimension: Greek statues of gods, Indian temple dances, Islamic calligraphy, Catholic cathedrals, Japanese Zen gardens and so on. Every major religious tradition has externalized its deep beliefs, traditional rituals, and existential experiences through various art forms. From mystical poetry that reveals an extraordinary vision, to tea ceremonies that make an everyday activity more spiritual, religion and beauty are always intertwined.

However, the contemporary modernist understanding of religion does not associate the religious with the creativity and freedom of art and beauty. It sees these as a sort of accidental side effect rather than intrinsic elements. Yet, religious art is used to express the ineffable. In other words, it tries to clarify truth through beauty. Religious artists are aware they can touch the hearts of people more easily with their art in order to convey their message. Beauty can therefore also lead people to truth. From this point of view, beauty and art form an unavoidable facet of religion.

To reiterate, the point is not that beliefs or rules of conduct are unimportant in religious contexts. Nor are they, by definition, completely subservient to concepts such as "experience" and "beauty." But even though beliefs and rules of conduct are often thrown into the mix, it is important to realize that religions consist of much more than just those two ingredients. Any attempt to analyze religion as a general phenomenon or to get a better grasp of a specific religious tradition must consider multiple dimensions, including the importance of profound experiences and the human impulse toward beauty.

All of this implies that we cannot reduce religion to these other dimensions either. Everything has its place in varying proportions: beliefs, precepts, experiences, and beauty provide a constant interplay in every religious tradition. Sometimes the emphasis lies on one, sometimes on the other. To gain a better understanding of religion, it will be necessary to map the relationships among all of these dimensions.

The fact that religions can never be reduced to a clear list of beliefs, the fact that their rules are constantly in motion, and the fact that core tenets keep being expressed in novel ways have a lot to do with their internal structure as well. It is generally assumed that religions are structured hierarchically and that some priestly class instructs adherents what to believe and how to live. Yet, this view is also difficult to justify when we have a closer look at the ways in which religions are actually lived. They do not necessarily involve a top-down chain of command—on the contrary. Hence, this will be the theme of the second chapter.

Myth #2

Religions Are Structured Hierarchically

To indicate the official, hierarchical character of religions, contemporary English has coined the phrase "organized religion." Yet in reality, there are few things as unorganized, muddled and unstructured as religious traditions. Whether we speak of Hinduism, Islam, Taoism, Judaism, African Ifa, or the shamanism of indigenous First Nations, none of these traditions has a central authority who determines the one, correct interpretation of their faith. They are all highly decentralized religions, and we could easily expand the list with many others from all corners of the world.

So, if there are more exceptions to the norm than exemplars, perhaps it is time we saw the supposed "norms" as exceptions. Differently put, when trying to get a better grasp of the underlying structure of various religions, the premise that they are generally *not* hierarchical tends to be a more helpful starting point.

A very good example is "Hinduism." The term embraces such an enormous diversity of traditions that it is quite nonsensical to seek unity within this multiplicity by trying to delineate some hierarchical structure. It is therefore worth taking a closer look at the lack of centralization within the Hindu traditions.

On Hinduism's indefinability and what this suggests regarding the lack of hierarchy

The standard definitions of "Hinduism" usually emphasize from the outset that there is no binding faith shared by all adherents. As a result, on reference sites aimed at a general audience, we can often read sentences such as: "Unlike most other religions, Hinduism has no single founder, no single scripture, and no commonly agreed upon set of teachings," or: "Hindus can choose to be polytheistic, pantheistic, panentheistic, pandeistic, henotheistic, monotheistic, monistic, agnostic, atheistic or humanist. Ideas about all the major issues of faith and lifestyle (…) are subjects of debate, not dogma."[27] Thus, Hinduism is an extreme example of what was set forth in the previous chapter.

Anyone who delves deeper into academic works in search of an illuminating definition will likewise be disappointed. In 2005, Professor J.E. Llewellyn took the time to compile an academic reader with various essays on this issue entitled *Defining Hinduism*. The introduction states quite bluntly: "So this is the problem: Hinduism has been variously and confusingly defined, where it has been defined at all."[28] Despite the title of the book, it does not eventually conclude on a solid definition of Hinduism, acceptable to all experts. On the contrary, a large part of the essays describe precisely why Hinduism is "by definition" indefinable.

Also, the word "Hindu" was not originally used to refer to "the adherents of Hinduism" at all. Rather, the word "Hindu" was a geographical and cultural designation. Persians and Muslims used it for many centuries as a descriptor of the people who lived beyond the Indus River (seen from their own region of origin). It is not entirely clear when the word "Hindu" was first used to refer to the religious identity of certain communities, but we do know for certain that it gradually took on an increasingly stronger religious connotation over the course of the colonization period. It is therefore only from the nineteenth century onwards that we see the word "Hinduism" commonly referring to a specific religion, as it starts occupying a prominent place in the texts of British academics, colonials, and missionaries.[29]

Consequently, there is a heated debate among scholars of Hinduism concerning the origin of "Hinduism" as a concept. Some argue it is merely a colonial and academic invention because the umbrella term "Hinduism" refers to such an enormous range of disparate beliefs and lifestyles that it eventually ceases to have any value as a category. From their perspective, it was mainly colonial rulers who wanted to unify a plethora of different traditions at all costs. Others argue that, no matter how great its variety, there still is a certain coherent whole that we could name "Hinduism" — not in the least because many Hindus today also use the word (or certain equivalents). The latter group of scholars often refers to the millennia-old texts of the Vedas as the historical basis of the ritual and theological core of Hinduism. But that view is criticized in return because it construes Hinduism as a scriptural religion (analogous with Christianity) even though, in many respects, scriptures are not central to many Hindu traditions. For example, as was already alluded to in the previous chapter, many Hindus have no idea what the Vedas convey, and their content often does not play any major role in the concrete, daily expressions of Hinduism. After all, the ritual traditions and ways of life that today are referred to as expressions of Hinduism are often a matter of orthopraxy and not of orthodoxy.[30] Thus, it is sometimes suggested that we mistakenly come to set a Brahminic perspective as the norm of Hinduism when we consistently focus on the Vedas, while many Hindus, past and present, do not identify with this Brahminic approach.

However, we do not need to lose ourselves in this particular debate, for the simple fact that it evokes a lot of discussion eventually emphasizes the point I am making: apparently, it is enormously difficult to figure out what exactly unites the various Hindu traditions. Even those who perceive it as a coherent whole will also indicate that a profound pluralism is one of the essential characteristics of Hinduism. Some of them even argue that the acceptance of multiplicity is the *only* element of unity.[31]

Leaving the definitional problems aside, we can return to the theme of this chapter since all of this is very relevant when we ask ourselves how "hierarchical" Hinduism is. Apparently, no single center of authority is capable of determining what Hinduism is or is not. There is no religious institution that can draw the exact boundaries. There is no religious ladder that we can easily climb to get to the top to enquire about "the most official version" of Hinduism. So, if we describe Hinduism as a religion, we need to keep in mind that it is a religion without a hierarchical structure, or at least without a defined religious institution which has the power to impose certain teachings on *all* followers of the religion. There is no central authority who can determine which ideas are within the established teachings and which are outside of it, or who can determine which precepts one should uphold in a "properly Hindu" way of life. In other words: within Hinduism it is difficult to determine what is mainstream and what is peripheral. It is all just a matter of perspective.

When we talk about hierarchy and Hinduism, many people will of course quickly refer to the caste system. However, even that system of social stratification needs a lot of nuances to be properly understood. The complex reality of the caste system is oversimplified by the common depiction of four castes (priests, warriors, merchants, workers) and marginalized outcastes. After all, the caste system is a very extensive, layered classification with thousands of subgroups. Those subgroups not only determine one's place in society, but sometimes additionally provide one with a social and economic network (not unlike guilds). Also, the caste system did not always have such a prominent place within Hindu communities as it has in recent centuries. Nor is it true that everyone belonging to the brahmin (priestly) caste, by definition, performs religious functions. And vice versa: some temple rituals in India are performed by people who are not brahmins.[32]

We must also question to what extent the caste system should be described as a *religious* hierarchy which is specifically prescribed by "Hinduism." On the one hand, there are several examples of influential Hindu movements that oppose the caste system,[33] and on the other hand, the caste system is also upheld among many Indian Christians, Muslims, Buddhists, and Sikhs. All in all, it is simply part and parcel of the wider culture, and as such, it is both upheld *and* criticized by (certain segments of) all the religions in the region.

Nevertheless, in attempts to emphasize the specifically Hindu character of the caste system, reference is often made to the verses of a short Vedic hymn, and to a few passages from the Manusmriti. But to what extent is it truly important that it is possible to unearth such scriptural references? Why would a short excerpt from some ancient text provide the unavoidable evidence that the caste system is unquestionably a *religious* hierarchy? If that is self-evident, perhaps we should also consider categorizing contemporary racism as a quintessential religious phenomenon. After all, the roots of contemporary racism can partly be traced to Christian debates about whether the "pagans" of "primitive societies" had a soul or not. At the start of the colonial period, these debates were conducted with great intensity. Another example is the biblical justification of slavery by American slaveholders who portrayed Africans as the descendants of Ham, a cursed son of Noah. In later centuries, however, the theological underpinnings of racism shifted toward a more biological and sociological underpinning. The racist hierarchy that got engrained in European and American culture became less justified by "the will of God" and was increasingly seen as "a natural fact." Black and brown people were no longer considered to be physically and culturally "underdeveloped" in comparison with the "superior" white people because they were "created" that way, but because they belonged to other "races." Yet, when racism still results in a lot of social hierarchy in contemporary society, it is never described as a *religious* hierarchy, while the caste system somehow is. Of course, it would be absurd to completely ignore every religious element from the caste system, but the opposite is equally absurd. It is too entrenched in the various social, political, and economic power relations of Indian society to simply portray it as "a religious phenomenon."

Above all, whatever the influence of religion on the caste system, it should be clear what it certainly is *not*. The caste system is *not* an "ecclesiastical" hierarchy that defines "the official doctrine of Hinduism." It is a complex social stratification that affects the ins and outs of a lot of dynamics in society, but it is *not* part of a defined religious institution. Again, such an institution simply does not exist in the multitude of traditions which are referenced by the umbrella-term "Hinduism."

Why Christianity is not contained within the Church

Anyone looking for a contrast to the total decentralization of Hindu traditions will probably point toward Christianity. If there is one religion whose hierarchical character seems obvious to many, it is this two-thousand-year-old tradition, and the institution which spontaneously comes to mind is the Catholic Church.

Obviously, the hierarchical nature of the Catholic Church is hard to deny, but that institution is an exception among the larger religious traditions. After all, it is extremely difficult to cite other examples of a hierarchical and centralistic institution, which for nearly two millennia had considerable influence over a large group of adherents concerning what should and should not demarcate the essence of their faith.

What is more, even within Christianity, the Catholic Church is an exception. The picture changes substantially as soon as we have a look at the Eastern and Oriental churches. These are commonly referred to as "Orthodox Christianity."[34] On the one hand, we can find relatively similar organizational structures within Orthodox Christianity because patriarchs, bishops, and priests occupy certain positions of power. On the other hand, Eastern Orthodox Christianity includes many different churches, which are all autonomous. These independent churches are largely determined by geographical, cultural, and linguistic elements. There is a Russian Orthodox Church, a Romanian Orthodox Church, a Greek Orthodox Church, a Bulgarian Orthodox Church and so on. The Ecumenical Patriarchate of Constantinople, the seat of the Orthodox Church in the Turkish territories, likes to see itself as the *primus inter pares*, since Constantinople (present-day Istanbul) used to be the capital of the Eastern Roman Empire. However, this patriarchy essentially has no authority over the other Orthodox churches. At regular intervals they have emphasized their independence quite clearly. On top of it, this does not even consider the Oriental Orthodox Churches, such as the Ethiopian Orthodox Tewahedo Church, the Armenian Apostolic Church, the Coptic Orthodox Church of Alexandria and so on. The Ecumenical Patriarch of Constantinople does not have any authority over these whatsoever.

Subsequently, when we have a look at the various branches of Protestant Christianity, we are once again confronted with complete decentralization. The dividing lines between the different Protestant denominations are determined by all kinds of theological discussions, social upheaval, migration movements and political tensions. Given their enormous variety, it is almost impossible to group them into well-defined clusters with a few simple but defining characteristics. They can only be mapped historically by tracing their moment of inception and by studying how exactly they were opposed to or aligned with various other groups of their time and place. As such, there is absolutely no umbrella structure that is capable of dictating to these various communities how they should organize themselves. As a counterpoint, one could perhaps refer to the World Council of Churches of which many Protestant churches are members (along with the Orthodox churches). This council meets about every ten years, but these gatherings are merely intended to network and exchange ideas on all kinds of topics. As such, they show no similarities to, for example, the Vatican councils of the Catholic Church, where official doctrines are laid down.

Thus, when we consider the three major branches of Christianity in their entirety, the conclusion is that Christianity, viewed as a whole, is not hierarchically structured either. None of the communities within the three main branches can force its religious supremacy on the others.

All of this becomes even clearer when we take a last step outside those three big branches. After all, the Archbishop of Canterbury has absolutely nothing to say about, for example, the Jehovah's Witnesses. Nor can the Pope exert power over the Church of the Last Testament, the group that formed around Sergei Anatolyevich Torop. This former policeman calls himself Vissarion and claims to be an incarnation of Christ. He has gathered several thousand followers in a remote corner of Siberia. The authorities within the older, better known and more established churches will of course dismiss such groups and spiritual leaders as "unchristian" excesses, but people who belong to these movements do see them as the only true *Christian* teaching. Purely sociologically speaking, they are therefore a part of Christianity, and consequently a very explicit example of the fact that besides a centralizing tendency, there is additionally a decentralizing tendency in Christianity.

Of course, many churches and Christian groups might *internally* be highly hierarchical. The Catholic Church certainly is not the only example in that regard. The same is true of the Orthodox Churches, and among Protestants we need only refer to Anglicanism, which in many respects is very similar to Catholicism—albeit with the

British monarch at the head. Yet, even this is not applicable across the board. We can easily identify Christian groups which organize themselves in an egalitarian manner and which do not recognize a priestly class. This is the case, for example, in some Quaker communities. These Quakers assume that the divine light is hidden in every human being and, consequently, that all believers carry "priesthood" within them. For this very reason, the meetings of some Quaker communities do not follow a specific course and participants are allowed to speak spontaneously when the inner divine light inspires them to do so.

Are we talking about religious hierarchy or merely human communal organization?

I certainly do not mean to insinuate that religious institutions seldom contain hierarchies. There certainly is an abundance of hierarchy in many religious contexts. I already gave plenty of examples.[35] However, that does not mean that religions in themselves are, by definition, centralized, top-down structures. A few comparisons may offer additional clarification in this regard. For example, while many businesses are organized very hierarchically, we do not consider the ideology of liberalism, as a whole, to be something "exceptionally hierarchical." Also, while all current democratic nation-states are centrally organized (with governments, parliaments, and so on), that does not mean we cannot think in a nuanced way about the balance between self-determination and hierarchy within societies that organize power relations through democratic processes. Similarly, although Stalin's Russia was very authoritarian, Marxist or communist ideologies do not by definition lead to hierarchical political structures, as is exemplified by the far-reaching plea for decentralization of anarcho-syndicalism.

During my discussion of the seventh myth about religion and the hierarchical elements of secular contexts, I shall delve a little deeper into these matters. For now, however, a simple observation will suffice. People unite for all kinds of social, economic, and political reasons, and constantly try to construe structures that can rally together various communities. This inevitably leads to the development of a wide range of organizations. Even if we offer some counterexamples of highly egalitarian democratic organizations, generally speaking, most of our institutions are organized hierarchically, to a greater or lesser extent.

As such, there seems to be no reason why this would be any different in religious contexts. Here too, it is possible to find some highly egalitarian democratic organizations, but the vast majority of religious institutions are organized hierarchically, to a greater or lesser extent. Hierarchy is thus by no means a specific feature of "religiosity." It is a specific characteristic of human community building.

Hence, when religious communities, groups, and institutions are hierarchically structured, there seems to be little difference with other non-religious communities, groups, and institutions. In this respect, one of the most striking examples is perhaps the Eastern Orthodox Christian Churches. As was already indicated, they largely correspond to the hierarchical structures of the (Greek, Russian, Romanian, etc.) nation-states in which they were founded.

When we consequently acknowledge that religions are not any more hierarchical than other forms of human interaction, we can proceed to wonder what the underlying structures of this social phenomenon truly are. If we agree that religions are not, by definition, construed by a priestly top layer, how then do they in fact develop?

A different look at the structure and development of religions

If one tries to trace the development of some particular religions over the centuries, one often finds lineages of master-disciple relationships. Spiritual masters, who immersed themselves in different facets of their religious tradition, come to be regarded as people who have a lot of wisdom to share, and therefore attract a group of disciples. Once some of these disciples demonstrate sufficient spiritual depth, they too can become recognized as masters, gather students around them and pass on their tradition (in a more or less modified form). In all its simplicity, this "basic structure" is extremely determinative for the traditional transmission of religious ideas and practices.

The centrality of this "structure" is visible through the huge amount of effort that is often put into recording the "chains" of spiritual transmission. Within all sorts of religious movements and communities, there is a codified remembrance of certain masters and how they passed on and contributed to the tradition. Just a few examples of these are the *parampara* ("continuing succession") of gurus among Hindus and Jains, the *kechimyaku* ("bloodline") of senseis in Zen Buddhism, the *silsilas* ("chains") of sheikhs in the Islamic mystic brotherhoods, and the tradition of *semikhah* ("leaning on") among rabbis in Judaism.

How adherents of a religion engage with those spiritual "family trees" can vary greatly. Sometimes the chains of transmission are formally written down in elaborate lists, and sometimes they are part of oral traditions which commemorate them in chants and prayers. Sometimes they are an especially important indication of one's spiritual development, and sometimes they are central in determining one's ritual authority.

In many traditions, specific historical segments of those spiritual family trees are of great importance. An explicit example thereof is the list of the first twelve great spiritual leaders of Iranian Shiism, which can be traced directly to Ali, the son-in-law of the Prophet Muhammad. Another example is the chain of transmission of the ten gurus of Sikhism, which concludes with a voluminous book called the *Guru Granth Sahib* ("the Master Guru Book") and which is therefore regarded as the final "guru."

Since masters are generally considered to have a "higher" status than their students, we could of course regard master-disciple relationships as a hierarchical structure. However, two important nuances are relevant here. First, this hierarchy is usually based on charisma and does not denote a position of power. In general, the students voluntarily commit themselves to the master. They feel a great awe for the wisdom of the master and therefore wish to receive his or her teaching. As such, their relationship usually is not a matter of imposed authority. Second, the hierarchical character of the master-disciple relationship strongly depends on the way in which the masters wield their position. There can be a lot of difference between individuals; some masters place themselves on a pedestal and expect great docility from their students, while others can be very humble and emphasize the essential equality of their students. So, when I refer to master-disciple relationships, it indicates an underlying structure that is not necessarily determined by an acute power imbalance. They can be hierarchical *or* egalitarian.

Ultimately, this type of relationship does not differ much from the traditional way in which arts and crafts have been passed on: a master initiates a pupil and trains him until he knows all the tricks of the trade. Subsequently the pupil takes the master's place and puts his own stamp on the art form. In these relationships of transference, the concept of "hierarchy" also does not seem very appropriate. Essentially, it is a matter of "sharing skills and mastery" and not of "bossing around." In that regard, it is not surprising that, in many cultures, the terms used to express respect for spiritual masters, such as "sensei" and "guru," are the same as those used for masters of arts and crafts.

All of this might not sound astonishing, but it is important nonetheless. It means that religions are not primarily *construed* by an institutionalized priestly class that, from the outset, pours the religion into a specific mold. Rather, religions organically *grow* in different directions like molds, through an enormous variety of (sometimes more and sometimes less formalized) master-disciple relationships.

What is more, religious institutions which have major influence over a large segment of their particular tradition often develop out of such a master-disciple relationship. When a master gathers a group around him, this direct relationship is often sufficient to maintain unity within the group. However, after a couple of generations, the community is sometimes formalized owing to the loss of this foundational relationship. Buddha, for example, had no intention of founding "Buddhism." Rather, he was one of the many spiritual masters of his time who proclaimed specific views based on religious concepts that were contemporary to him (and which can therefore also be found in all kinds of Hindu denominations). In various forms, his spiritual teachings were widely disseminated throughout Southeast Asia. His ideas also found their way to Tibet. Yet, the well-known hierarchically institutionalized tradition of Tibetan Buddhism, headed by the Dalai Lama, did not emerge until about two millennia after the Buddha. Moreover, it took a long time for contemporary Tibetan Buddhism to institutionalize. After all, the first Dalai Lama was not bestowed with this title until about a hundred years after his death. In his own time, he was seen as a spiritual master of one specific Buddhist school. It was not until the fifth Dalai Lama that this position was assigned as the highest religious and political position in Tibet.

Christianity can also serve as an illustration, for both Jesus and his apostles considered themselves to be Jews. Jesus proclaimed his message in synagogues and went on a pilgrimage to the temple in Jerusalem. Building an ecclesiastical institution was certainly not his goal. In all likelihood, the idea never occurred to him. Partly because of the persecution of the early Christians, Jesus' followers quickly grouped together as a distinct community, yet the formalization of Christian churches as delineated institutions did not really begin until Christianity became the Roman state religion in the fourth century.

The fact that master-disciple relationships are central to the development of religions is therefore of great importance if we wish to map the structure of the various religious traditions. Religion is not just a matter of "doctrinal clashes" and "schisms," as it is often assumed. To a much greater extent, it is in fact a matter of "spiritual variations" and "personal interpretations." This also immediately clarifies why, as explained in the previous chapter, the beliefs and precepts of specific religious traditions cannot be neatly defined, and why we can find enormous diversity within each of these traditions.

Yet, let us also not elevate the various forms of master-disciple relationships to an absolute criterion. Although they serve as a basic building block of the development of many traditions, that does not mean that they are the one and only element that explains everything. The growth of religions is also strongly determined by their cultural embedment, for example. When religious ideas, practices and ways of life spread across regions, communities, and societies, they never do so in a vacuum. They always mix with the already-present art forms, rituals, and stories.

Suppose, for example, that there is a community in which people mainly use songs to bring their favored mythological stories to life. When those mythological stories, for whatever reason, seep into a community where dance is a respected art form, they will soon be turned into choreographies. This is a spontaneous and natural process, but the eventual result is an undeniable expansion of this specific religious tradition. Where previously only devotional songs were a ritual part of the tradition, sacred dancing has now been added.

We could call this "the accumulation of traditions."[36] Sometimes this can be resultant from conscious interventions by a priestly class or an elite group that wishes to push the religious community in a specific direction, but for the most part it concerns practices, rituals, and customs that develop organically from popular devotional expressions. In the Christian tradition, for example, the liturgy of the Eucharist is strongly determined by the ecclesiastical institutions. Yet, the popular devotion to Mary has for centuries served as the inspiration for countless chapels, pilgrimages, processions, chants, and prayers. They were, and often still are, much more decisive in the daily experience of Christians. As a result, 66 percent of all Catholic shrines in Europe are dedicated to Mary.[37] So, even though Christianity is originally based on the teachings of Jesus who called God his Father, the accumulation of the tradition additionally resulted in a widespread spirituality in which his Mother played the central role.

Moreover, the accumulation of traditions is not only the result of ritual or theological additions internal to the traditions themselves. Often, these are a result of exchanges *between* traditions. In this respect, the influence of a hierarchical authority is even less important since people with a more dogmatic view of religion are generally more averse to outside influence. However, precisely because such a thing is seldom imposed, and instead is generally an organic and spontaneous event, it is oftentimes impossible to determine exactly how some religious phenomena originated. Once more, the Christian Marian devotion offers a good example thereof, since, for centuries, it has been accompanied by the use of a rosary, a string of beads used as an aid in Marian prayers. One can find such prayer beads all over the world and the rosary is, likely, a Christian appropriation of a religious practice that already existed in other places. As Prof. Marina Warner describes in her book on the Christian cult of Mary:

> The chain of beads or knops originated in Brahmanic India, where it is still current in the worship of Vishnu and Shiva.

Through Hinduism its use spreads to Buddhism, and later to Islam, where it is referred to as early as the ninth century. (...) Although the exact point and date of entry of the rosary into western Christendom is not known, the crusaders are generally given the credit for spreading a habit picked up from their Moslem adversaries. But (...) the practice of counting one's prayers was known in England before the first crusade and may therefore have arisen spontaneously, or been imported by pilgrims to the holy land.[38]

The quote is sufficiently nuanced, but we can nevertheless add that the Islamic *tasbih* may not have come from the *malas* of the Hindus or Buddhists, but rather was inspired by the knotted prayer chords of Orthodox Christianity, used by the desert fathers in the early centuries of Christianity. So, we do not know exactly how it happened, but one thing is certain: religious practices from one tradition were frequently copied by other traditions.

The accumulation of religious stories: Barlaam and Josaphat

Religious stories are likewise often appropriated from other traditions. A good example is the legend of Barlaam and Josaphat. The story of these two Christian saints was extremely popular in the late Middle Ages. As such, it can be encountered in Greek, Latin, Arabic, Georgian, Slavic, Ethiopian, and Armenian manuscripts. It can be summarized as follows:

The Indian king Abenner built a gigantic palace so that his son Josaphat would never have to go outside and thus would never encounter the Christian monks who were proliferating in India at the time. After all, the court astrologers had predicted that Josaphat would become an honored ascetic and thus obtain "a higher kingdom." But Josaphat was very curious by nature and wanted to see more of the world. His father eventually relented, causing Josaphat to take to the streets, where he was confronted with a blind man, an injured man, and an old man who was approaching death. The startled Josaphat did not know how to deal with the suffering he had seen. However, the Christian monk Barlaam had a vision of the young Josaphat. He changed his clothes, entered the palace, and shared his Christian beliefs with Josaphat. The young man was deeply moved by what he had heard and asked to be baptized. When the king learned that his son had been baptized, he tried to change his mind by sending him beautiful women and seducing him to earthly pleasures. However, Josaphat resisted all temptations. His father therefore divided the kingdom in two and left one part to Josaphat. Showing ideal Christian leadership, people migrated from King Abenner's kingdom to Josaphat's. When the king realized what happened, he repented. For a while they ruled together, but when the king finally died, Josaphat chose to visit Barlaam once more and spend the latter part of his life as a monk.

For anyone who has the least bit of acquaintance with Buddhist mythology it is crystal clear: in many ways, this hagiography is an almost literal copy of the Buddha's life story. However, medieval European Christians, in general, had never heard of the Buddha. It was simply assumed that the story was originally recorded by Saint John of Damascus. It was not until the nineteenth century that the discovery of several manuscripts brought to the fore how the classical life story of the Buddha had found its way to Europe and became Christianized through various adaptations.[39]

The accumulation of traditions thus raises even more questions about contemporary views on religion. It is often thought that the beliefs, mythological stories, and ritual practices of religions are closely guarded by a priestly class, and that they spread throughout the world because they are imposed by a priestly class. While such dynamics can undoubtedly arise, they are by no means the norm. Religions grow from below as much as they are imposed from above.

Again, I am certainly not arguing in this chapter that hierarchical religious institutions are of no importance. My intention is merely to clarify the pointlessness of singling out this specific aspect. Anyone who really wants to understand the structure and growth of religious traditions will always have to keep an eye on *all* contributing aspects. Thus, in addition to institutionalization, we must pay equal attention to the patterns of spiritual transmission through master-disciple relationships and to the cumulative effects on tradition through cultural exchanges and embedment. On top of it, I even failed to mention the most basic structure of all, which is so obvious that I did not feel the need to discuss it in more detail: the way in which family ties ensure that parents pass on all kinds of stories, ideas, and habits to their children. Needless to say, we must also always remain aware of the fact that all of these elements are constantly intertwined.

To those who have ever taken the trouble to investigate a specific religious tradition in depth and breadth, this more holistic approach will probably seem self-evident, but as obvious as it might seem to some, culturally speaking it is not. After all, this holistic view inevitably sounds the death knell for the myth about religion that was discussed in this chapter. Religions are not permanent hierarchical structures at all. They are a constantly evolving and dynamic set of relationships.

Religions Can Be Clearly Distinguished, Based on Their Beliefs, Rules, and Structures

Since religions are not determined by beliefs, since rules of conduct rarely apply to all adherents and since most traditions have no hierarchical structure, it should not come as a surprise that religions cannot always be clearly distinguished from one another. While discussing the first myth, I referred to the fact that we can find Hindu gods in Thai, Buddhist temples. In China we can also come across shrines where images of the Buddha, Confucius, and Lao Tzu stand on the same altar,[40] while in Japan "many visit Buddhist temples as well as pray for luck and happiness at Shinto shrines," as an article in the *Japan Times* once described it.[41]

Those are just a few examples from countries where Buddhism is widely practiced, but the same phenomena can be witnessed in the most diverse religious contexts. In this respect it is worthwhile to have a deeper look at the areas in Pakistan and India where Islam and Hinduism intersect. The former religion is known for its strict monotheism, and the latter for its profound polytheism, however, cross-pollination between the two is quite commonplace.

On the religious mingling around the Indus

A first example of the overlap between Islamic and Hindu traditions is the annual festival at the mausoleum of Lal Shahbaz Qalandar, who is the most important Islamic saint in Pakistan. Many Hindus also pay tribute to him by dancing in the streets and praying at his grave. After all, Hindus from the region see Lal Shahbaz Qalandar as the (re)incarnation of Jhulelal, the God of the Indus River. Yet, Muslims also use Jhulelal as an epithet in the many devotional songs they dedicate to the saint.

Conversely, we can just as well encounter Indian Muslims in Hindu temples. For example, in Maharashtra province, Muslims participate in the worship of the god Khandoba, an incarnation of Shiva. The traditional horses at the center of the annual festival in Jejuri (where the worship of Khandoba is most prominent) are not only cared for by a Muslim family but also led by Muslims during the processions.[42]

In one of her books, the renowned Indologist and Sanskritist Wendy Doniger describes how one can see a religious entanglement not only in people's daily devotional practices, but also in classical literature:

> Much of the poetry written by Muslims (...) begins with the Islamic invocation of Allah but goes on to express Hindu content or makes use of Hindu forms, Hindu imagery, Hindu terminology. In return, the sixteenth-century Bangla text entitled *The Ocean of the Nectar of Bhakti*, by the [Hindu] theologian Rupagoswamin, tells the life of Krishna in a form modeled on a Sufi romance. The heroes of the Persian epic the *Shah Nama* and the Sanskrit *Mahabharata* interact in the *Tarikh-i-Farishta*, composed under the Mughals.[43]

Much classical poetry in India and Pakistan was similarly written by figures who can be described as "hybrid saints." After all, in the cases of several highly revered spiritual figures from this region, it is not always clear whether they were Muslim, Hindu or both. A particularly striking case is Lalleshwari, also known as Lal Ded. She was a fourteenth-century saint from Kashmir who, according to the traditional stories about her life, walked around naked, because she was fully enraptured by her unification with the divine and stopped caring about her worldly status. Even today, her poems are well known throughout the region and have inspired many songs. In the twentieth century, however, Pakistani professors tried to prove that she was a Muslim, while their Indian colleagues argued she was a Hindu. The fact that both groups were able to do so convincingly shows how impossible it is to give a definite answer to the question. Yet, for hundreds of years, the people who recited her verses did not seem to care.[44]

I could also refer to someone like the seventeenth-century Sarmad Kashani. This mystical philosopher and spiritual teacher of Dara Shikoh (a great-grandchild of the famous Mughal Emperor Akbar) not only mixed Islamic ideas with Hindu elements, but he was, originally, an Armenian Jew.

The unitarian religion of Akbar

The Islamic Mughal Emperor Akbar is known for his Din-i-Ilahi. This refers to his attempt to integrate all the religious and spiritual ideas of his time and combine them into one single teaching. Although this Din-i-Ilahi, in a certain sense, was retained within the palace walls, his pluralistic attitude was important for something we could describe (anachronistically, albeit) as the interfaith dialogue of his time. He held regular meetings at his court where scholars and preachers from different traditions entered into discussions with one another and displayed both their rhetorical talents and their theological wisdom. Akbar also reportedly made statements such as: "The wisdom of *vedanta* [a monistic Hindu tradition] is the same wisdom of *tasawwuf* [Islamic spirituality and mysticism]" and "All traditions are either equally true or equally illusory." Because of this mindset, he also immersed himself deeply in Christianity. As Wendy Doniger explains in her book *The Hindus*, the Christian missionaries found his pluralistic and eclectic attitude difficult to grasp: "He flirted to such a degree [with Christianity] that the Portuguese missionaries congratulated themselves that he was on the brink of converting—until they realized that he continued to worship at mosques (and, on occasion, at Hindu temples, as well as participate in Parsi fire rituals). Here, not for the first or last time, Muslim and Hindu pluralism ran up against Christian intolerance."[45]

The nineteenth-century Shirdi Sai Baba is worth mentioning as well.[46] In Maharashtra, the region of India in which he lived, one can often find his image on amulets in taxis, on posters, and in temple sculptures. During his lifetime, both Muslims and Hindus regarded him as a spiritual teacher. It is said that he counseled his Muslim students with verses from the Qur'an and his Hindu students with verses from the Bhagavad Gita.

The fifteenth-century Kabir is yet another example. Not only can we find both Hindu and Islamic influences in his popular mystical poetry, some of these poems have also been included in the Guru Granth Sahib. The same is true of some poems composed by the thirteenth-century Islamic mystic Fariduddin Ganjshakar. Yet, as I noted in the previous chapter, the Guru Granth Sahib is considered to be the last "Guru" of the Sikhs. This holy book not only contains the core doctrine of Sikhism but it is also literally placed at the center of community rituals. It should not come as a surprise, however, that Sikhs included texts from other traditions in the Guru Granth Sahib, for when we take a closer look at the teachings of Guru Nanak (the first Guru of the Sikhs), we will see that they were full of elements that either stem from Islam (such as the emphasis on the unity of God) or from Hindu traditions (such as the emphasis on the principle of spiritual liberation).

In the past as well as today, the exact tradition to which these "hybrid saints" adhered seemed rather irrelevant to the general public. What mattered was their spiritual charisma and the inspiration their words offered to people. They were honored for the greatness of their soul, not for the fact that they belonged to one particular tradition.

How several religions embrace other traditions

The teachings of such "hybrid saints" often include the idea that "all the earlier prophets and sages conveyed a universal message" or that "there is a common spiritual truth underpinning every tradition." This type of thought can take different forms and might be developed to differing degrees by various groups, but the core of the message is promoted quite frequently.

Since our contemporary understanding of religion is generally based on the first two myths (religions consist of specific beliefs and behaviors, which are defined by hierarchical structures) it is sometimes thought that this manner of thinking arose only recently. It is seen as a hallmark of "modern" spiritual teachers who have left the "straitjacket of religion" and are therefore free enough to discard dogmatic beliefs and discover the underlying deeper truths revealed by different traditions. However, it is a fairly typical vision that has popped up regularly throughout history.

For example, the idea was expressed very explicitly at the very first World's Parliament of Religions in 1893, which was one of the first grand international interfaith gatherings. It is often referred to as one of the first occasions in which Western intellectuals and academics conversed with representatives from different religious traditions on equal footing. The influential Vivekananda took the floor as a representative of Hinduism and did so with these famous words:

> I am proud to belong to a religion which has taught the world both tolerance and universal acceptance. We believe not only in universal toleration, but we accept all religions as true. (...) I will quote to you, brethren, a few lines from a hymn which I remember to have repeated from my earliest

boyhood, which is every day repeated by millions of human beings: "As the different streams having their sources in different paths which men take through different tendencies, various though they appear, crooked or straight, all lead to Thee."[47]

Vivekananda's words were by no means innovative. Such beliefs were not only widespread in India, but particular emphasis was placed on them by his own guru, Ramakrishna, who is known for statements like these:

The important thing is to reach the roof. You can reach it by stone stairs or by wooden stairs or by bamboo steps or by a rope. You can also climb up by a bamboo pole. (...) One should not think, "My religion alone is the right path and other religions are false." God can be realized by means of all paths. It is enough to have sincere yearning for God. Infinite are the paths and infinite the opinions.[48]

Some two centuries earlier, Guru Gobind Singh, the tenth guru of the Sikhs, wrote the following verses:

The temple and the mosque are the same, there is no difference between a Hindu worship and Muslim prayer. (...) The Puranas of Hindus and the holy Qur'an of the Muslims depict the same reality.[49]

Even at that time, this was far from a surprising statement. After all, we can trace Gobind Singh's vision to the teachings of the very first Guru of the Sikhs, the previously quoted sixteenth-century Guru Nanak.

Even further back in time, and from an entirely different region, we can likewise refer to someone like the Prophet Muhammad. Admittedly, he is considered the seal of the prophets (the final prophet sent by God) in most Islamic denominations, yet this also implies that all other preceding prophets are accepted as equally legitimate. Muhammad clearly placed himself within an Abrahamic lineage. That is to say, he recognized the truthfulness of the teachings that were spread by Jewish prophets ever since Abraham, even including the figure of Christ as an important messenger. To quote just a few sentences from the Qur'an in this regard:

> Say, "We believe in God and in what was sent down to us and what was sent down to Abraham, Ishmael, Isaac, Jacob, and the Tribes, and what was given to Moses, Jesus, and all the prophets by their Lord. We make no distinction between any of them, and we devote ourselves to Him."[50]

When we take one further step back in time, we can also consider Manichaeism. From the third to the fifth century, it was one of the biggest "competitors" of the disparate religious movements that would eventually become the established churches of Christianity. Manichaeism is often overlooked because the portrayal of early Christian history generally identifies only three traditions: Judaism, Christianity, and the Greco-Roman philosophical and religious traditions. Yet for a long time, Manichaeism had a large following in the Mediterranean and the Middle East. Many church fathers therefore considered it necessary to refute and condemn the Manichaean beliefs in their texts. Nevertheless, it was a Christian group—albeit a group that relied on the teachings of Mani, who interpreted the message of Christ in such a way that it became an affirmation of all previous spiritual truths. Mani also saw himself as a prophet who affirmed the same ancient wisdom. This is evident from the *Shabuhragan*, one of the books in which Mani's teachings were recorded. Few fragments of that book have survived, but the eleventh-century Al-Biruni, who had access to the full manuscript, translated a passage from the introduction as follows:

> Wisdom and deeds have always from time to time been brought to mankind by the messengers of God. So in one age they have been brought by the messenger, called Buddha, to India, in another by Zarâdusht [Zarathustra] to Persia, in another by Jesus to the West. Thereupon this revelation has come down, this prophecy in this last age through me, Mânî, the messenger of the God of truth to Babylonia.[51]

Of course, such views never exist in a vacuum. They are linked to many other beliefs and ideas. Therefore, some religious leaders sometimes proclaimed conflicting doctrines. At certain times, they emphasized the unity between their insights and those of others before them, while at others they distanced themselves from specific views of particular spiritual groups who they confronted in their respective times and localities. Yet, contradictory or not, "witnessing the unity of religions" was regularly brought to the fore, and the followers of those religious leaders have often emphasized it as an important aspect of their teachings.

The fact that such notions of underlying unity are so common in various places and traditions throughout history makes it even more difficult to maintain that it is possible to neatly catalog the different religions anytime, anywhere. How exactly do we distinguish one tradition from another when it is inherently accepted that all other traditions are wholly compatible with all others? How can we draw a line between religions when some religions adhere to the principle that it is good to include elements from the other traditions in their own?

The further history of Manichaeism makes it clear just how complex all of this can become. Dr. Brent Nongbri summed it up as follows:

The story of Mani and his followers is not confined just to the ancient Mediterranean world. By the seventh century, followers of Mani had migrated into China, largely via the trade routes of the Silk Road. By the twelfth century, Manichaean groups were a well-established feature of the southeastern coastlands of China. These eastern Manichaean groups adopted many ideas from the Buddhists and Taoists with whom they interacted. A regular title for Mani in the Chinese literature is "Mani the Buddha of Light" (Moni guangfo), and other sources identify him as a reincarnation of Laozi, the reputed author of the Dao De Jing. Nevertheless, Jesus remained a key figure even for these Manichaeans, who at times seem to fully identify Jesus with the Buddha as Jesus-Buddha (Yishu fo). Indeed, as late as the thirteenth century, there is some evidence of a Manichaean group self-identifying to Mongol rulers (at the behest of none other than Marco Polo!) as Christians along with local Nestorian Christians. Thus, groups of Manichaeans were different entities in different contexts to different observers. They constituted a Christian heresy at Rome, they were the Christianity in Kellis, and in Chinese settings they appeared in a range of manifestations, from simply another type of Christian alongside the Nestorians of China to something like a Buddhist heresy.[52]

On multiple religious belonging

Since the beginning of the twenty-first century there is, in academic circles, a growing interest in what is called "multiple religious belonging." The term speaks for itself: it describes the way in which some people adhere to different religious traditions. This phenomenon, as well, is often portrayed as characteristic of our fluid and (post)modern times, based on the idea that far-reaching individualism makes people reluctant to remain within the boundaries of a single religion and allowing them to compose their personal spirituality. Sometimes this can be a matter of superficial "cafeteria religion," but it can also be the result of sincere attempts to become familiar with multiple traditions from the inside out, making people feel at home in more than one tradition.

The academic interest in multiple religious belonging should not come as a surprise since the concept seems to apply to a substantial segment of contemporary society.[53] We can come across all sorts of interesting combinations, such as Jubus (Jewish Buddhists) or the followers of the Santo Daime (a Christian community that incorporates Shamanic rituals involving the use of the hallucinogenic ayahuasca). In addition, a concept like multiple religious belonging can help to explicate the behavior of people who do not see themselves as members of a particular community, but who are, for example, inspired by new age literature and decorate their living room with elements from a diverse patchwork of traditions.

Ultimately, however, there is nothing new or exceptional about multiple religious belonging. As should be clear from the many examples offered in this chapter, it has been a regular phenomenon throughout history, and all over the world.

Furthermore, mixing traditions is not always a conscious process. Religious pluralism does not always arise because spiritual leaders explicitly try to incorporate elements from other religions. Neither is it always the result of individuals deliberately delving into multiple traditions, nor of separate communities intertwining through dialogue and exchange. Often, it is the unplanned consequence of a gradual process in which certain symbols, stories, concepts, ideas, rituals, and customs from one religion are absorbed into another. Usually such dynamics are called "syncretism." Although the term itself refers to the mixing of elements from different religions in general, it is often used more specifically for the "transformation" of certain religious elements—and these transformations abound just as well.

On the ubiquity of syncretism

One of the best-known examples of religious syncretism is Christmas. In all likelihood many of its ritual elements hail from shamanic customs, which were embedded in ancient European nature spiritualities in celebration of the winter solstice. Another well-known example is the way in which elements of the ancient Egyptian worship surrounding Isis, the mother goddess, became interwoven with Christianity through the cult of Mary. As a result, some contemporary depictions of Mary nursing Jesus still resemble first-century depictions of Isis.[54] A lesser-known example was mentioned in the previous chapter: the hagiographies of Barlaam and Josaphat were very popular among medieval Christians, although they were actually adaptations of Buddha's life story.

In other contexts, like the Haitian voodoo, the Brazilian candomblé and the Cuban Santeria, one can easily see that, during the colonization period, saints of European Christianity mingled with the gods and goddesses of African Ifa. Those traditions, characterized by trance rituals, are in turn reminiscent of Zar dances in Egypt, Gnawa rituals in Morocco, in which the Islamic tradition is fused with so-called animist elements from even older North-African traditions.

These last examples make it quite clear that it is not just a matter of religions intertwining with one another. Oftentimes, religions also cannot be neatly demarcated from phenomena such as "shamanism," "animism," "magic," or "witchcraft." It is often thought that such concepts do not belong within the boundaries of the better-known major religious traditions owing to their rejection by the mainstream adherents. That is not self-evident, however. For example, in the first chapter I indicated that British and Scottish Christians of the fifteenth, sixteenth and seventeenth centuries saw no discrepancies at all between their Christian faith, their animistic beliefs about the fairy world, and the fact that they frequently sought the help of witches who could communicate with spirits.

In other traditions we can also find other such complex, interwoven phenomena which are difficult to delineate. In order not to elaborate endlessly on this topic, I only refer briefly to amulets of the evil eye and the hand of Fatima. Many Muslims wear such amulets on their bodies or hang them on a door as a means to protect themselves from evil. Both symbols are often also combined on a necklace or ornament. After all, jealous stares (from humans as well as demons) are reflected back by the eye and the hand stops the negative energy from such gazes. However, both symbols are common throughout the entire Mediterranean since they have a long history which predates Islam, which can be traced to customs of magic and witchcraft from ancient Egypt and Mesopotamia. As a result, one can just as easily find such protective amulets among Middle Eastern Jews and Christians, who have connected these symbols to their own religious mythology.

Why fundamentalists do not exhibit the "pure" teachings of their tradition

From subjection to subtle influences, through creative entanglement, to far-reaching syncretism, all over the globe and throughout history, every religious tradition appears to be very flexible and dynamic. Those who want to find a theoretical "pureness" which can be clearly demarcated from all others, will be kept searching for a long time. After all, anyone who takes a closer look at any religious tradition will soon notice such "pure" teachings—completely independent and distinguishable from all other traditions—cannot be found. When we delve deeper into the history and cultural scope of any tradition, we will be confronted again and again with ideas that are exchanged, rituals that are adopted, texts that are forgotten, stories that are being adjusted, and symbols that are being added. As a result, the boundaries of specific traditions cannot always be neatly drawn.

Of course, there have always been fundamentalists who have tried to keep their religion as "pure" as possible. There is no shortage of people and groups of various religious traditions, contemporary and historical, who attempt to clearly define certain doctrines, who want to banish some rituals, who want to lay down a set of strict moral rules, and who write lengthy tracts to hereticate those who hold different opinions. However, even though such attempts aim to preserve the tradition in question with the utmost purity, in the end, they inevitably fail since they will always be just one strand among the many. Even if those attempts gained great authority because they were backed by certain elites, it still does not make them the obvious benchmark of a religion.[55] As has long been demonstrated, the will of the elites has rarely been a good indication of people's actual beliefs. "Vernacular religion" will always present a far more diverse picture.

As such, we should not take as fact the rhetoric of specific groups who make theological claims regarding how "pure" their religious adherence might be. Nor should we revert to the idea that religions are determined and guarded by hierarchical institutions. That was sufficiently debunked in the previous chapter. We must, however, consider the religious traditions in their broad diversity and recognize this simple sociological fact: religions mix. Not once in a while, but constantly. Not in a few places, but everywhere.

The many examples presented in this chapter show just how flexible the boundaries between different religions are. By presenting a good many of them, I hoped to demonstrate how one tradition is not always easily distinguished from another. We cannot refer to Christianity, Islam, Hinduism, Taoism, Buddhism, Judaism, Ifa, Baha'ism, Zoroastrianism or the shamanism of Native Americans as if they are self-evident, distinct entities of which we can neatly list all the elements they absolutely do or do not contain. The manifold ways in which people have experienced those traditions are simply too diverse to portray them as isolated monoliths.

All of this emphasizes just how untenable the first myth about religion is. For how strict can certain religious beliefs be, when ideas, symbols and stories from different traditions mix so easily? How rigorous are the precepts and rituals of religions, when practices which are heresies according to one community, became a standard part of life in another?

Clearly then, we need a different view on the demarcation and delineation of the different religious traditions.

A different look at religious boundaries: religion as "language"

When we speak of religions today, they are often described like products in a supermarket: packages of beliefs, rules of conduct, symbols, and rituals, which are offered by specific brands. These brands advertise their own particular product range: reincarnation in the package of one religion, a heaven in that of the other; prayer in the package of one religion, meditation in that of the other; priests in the package of one religion, rabbis in that of the other. Some brands additionally offer multiple variants of their merchandise, such as a Sunni version and a Shia version, or a Japanese Zen edition and a Thai Theravada edition. However, no elements are exchanged between the brands, let alone trade secrets. After all, each brand wants to outcompete the others, and obtain a monopoly in the religious market.

However, the first three chapters have shown that such a view of religion is impossible to maintain. Most religions do not have a straightforward "product," they are not "managed" like distinct companies, and their "merchandise" is constantly exchanged.

If we would like to achieve a better understanding of religion, it seems more apt to make a comparison to language. Such a comparison can clarify why the boundaries of different religions are so porous and fluid. For example, we know that languages can mix in many ways because of loan words (like the many English words in contemporary Hindi), because a complete "intermediate language" arose (like Creole), or because some people deliberately created a mixed language (like Esperanto). Similarly, religions can sometimes adopt specific rituals (like the use of prayer beads in different traditions), a complete "intermediate religion" can sometimes arise (like Sikhism), or some people might consciously create a syncretic religion (like the Din-i-Ilahi of the Mughal Emperor Akbar).

We also have little trouble with the concept of multilingualism. Not only do some people grow up in a family where several languages are spoken, all of us can also choose to learn an extra language. Likewise, multiple religious belonging should not be difficult to comprehend: some people grow up in a context where various traditions surround them on a daily basis and all of us can choose to delve into a tradition that we were not raised in. Of course, in the case of languages, our native language usually remains the one in which we are most proficient, and which comes to us most intuitively. Yet here again, we can easily find a similarity, for even when people convert, concepts from their "mother religion" often still influence their thinking.

Another parallel can be drawn with dialects. After all, a patchwork of dialects ensures great internal diversity within every language. The differences within dialects can sometimes be so profound that those who speak the same language no longer understand one another. Likewise, in a religion the diversity can be so great that the beliefs and practices of one group become incomprehensible to another. A Japanese Zen Buddhist has no idea how to perform the rituals in a Thai Theravada temple, and a Protestant Christian who is used to an extremely austere church building does not always feel at home among the many icons and statues of saints in a monastery of

Orthodox Christians.

We can likewise easily accept that languages are not "invented," "prescribed" or "imposed," but rather "originate," "grow," and "change." Even though certain reference books might determine the correct spelling, and even though the grammar rules of "standardized language" is laid down by linguists and taught by language instructors, we realize that languages are constantly evolving in people's daily communications. The same applies to religions: even if a specific religious community recognizes holy scriptures, and even if they have some sort of priestly class, their religion still continues to evolve in the daily experience of their faith.

Finally, just like there are fundamentalists in religions who want to keep their religion as "pure" as possible, there are also language purists in every linguistic area. This "purity" is not proclaimed by priests but preached by schoolteachers and sometimes even by nationalist political leaders who base their power on perpetuating a specific cultural identity. They often look down on certain dialects and slang, thus ignoring how much these variants are an undeniable part of the actual language diversity. They will similarly sometimes pretend the correct language rules have always been the same and that their language can only be spoken in one specific way. In the light of history, of course, this is nonsense. Middle English, for example, is recognizable for contemporary English speakers, but quite difficult to read. Let alone that people still speak in the manner of eleventh-century British people. Likewise, a gathering of the apostles in the early Christian communities would be unrecognizable to Christians today. To give but a few examples: the New Testament did not exist at all (and as such the first Christians were mainly familiar with the Jewish Torah); there was no mention of a central doctrinal concept like Trinity in the first two centuries of Christianity; and important Greco-Roman philosophical concepts, which were unknown to Jesus' disciples, had yet to be infused into Christianity by the Church Fathers.

> **Jesus was a Jew**
> Too often it is forgotten that Jesus explicitly placed himself within the Jewish traditions. He did not intend to establish a separate religion. In one of his books, the Benedictine exegete Benoît Standaert gave several examples of Jesus' Jewishness. At the end of that exposition, he added with a final chord: "Jesus is truly a Jew—more than we would imagine—and when it comes to marking the anniversary of his birth, we Christians are more Jewish than we realize. In Judaism boys celebrate becoming a year older on the anniversary of their circumcision rather than on their birthday. On the first of January, eight days after the Birth of Jesus, we continue to read the gospel of his circumcision and of his being given a name. Following good Jewish custom, then, the New Year does not begin on the day of Jesus' birth but eight days later."[56]

That does not mean, of course, that everything is completely incohesive and amorphous. Certain elements do bind a religion together, but these elements are always flexible. This too is akin to language: languages undoubtedly have a distinctiveness because of the conventions concerning their vocabulary and grammar, but these conventions are always subject to change as well.

In short, one can think of religions as languages which do not consist of vocabulary and grammar, but of symbols, rituals, stories, ideas, and ways of life. From this perspective, the inherent flexibility of religion becomes much easier to understand. The many examples in this chapter suddenly cease to be "peculiar exceptions," and instead become obvious demonstrations of lived religion. Although these symbols, rituals, stories, ideas, and ways of life determine the distinctiveness of a tradition, they are simultaneously always subject to change.

That being said, a comparison is, of course, just a comparison. In addition to the many similarities with language, one can probably also list some differences. However, this particular comparison allows us to approach religion from a different perspective and, at the end of this chapter, it also becomes clear why there is a great need to do so: the contemporary perception of religion is grossly inadequate. Anyone who digs a little deeper into one of the many religious traditions that enrich our world will find that the standard theoretical concepts are constantly turned upside down.

In the first three chapters I could therefore easily provide several examples which undermine the three main myths about religion. It would be possible to add many more examples which show again and again that religions cannot be reduced to beliefs or fixed rules of conduct; that they are not securely controlled by hierarchical institutions; and that they cannot always be clearly distinguished.

As such, this seems like a good moment to take a pause before moving on to the following four myths. This will allow us to take a step back in the proceeding interlude and ask some pertinent questions which are probably crossing the mind of the reader. Why is it so difficult to define religion when it has been studied for so long? Why do we assume that religion has certain characteristics, while those characteristics are absent in many traditions? And have people always had such a problematic view of religion, or is this a recent phenomenon?

Interlude

On the Definition, Origin, and Racist Dimensions of the Word "Religion"

Why we are not capable of properly defining religion

The facts, nuances and examples presented in the preceding chapters are rarely juxtaposed in the manner I have done so far. Once they are, it becomes apparent that important factors, which need to be kept in mind when trying to get a better grasp of religion, are consistently overlooked. Yet, when such intricacies are honestly and transparently discussed, it can start to feel uncomfortable because the word "religion" seems to slip through our fingers. As a result, a fundamental part of our worldview is suddenly jeopardized. Some might therefore feel that it would make sense to start searching for a precise definition of the term "religion" once more, in the hope of finding more solid ground.

However, as I already mentioned in the introduction, countless attempts to define religion have been made over the decades and none of them have been successful. Not a single definition ever grew into a generally accepted standard. In fact, one of the few widely shared ideas within the current academic field of religious studies is precisely that such a conclusive definition is not achievable. So, let us perhaps have a look at the various proposals that have already been offered and why they fell short.

The majority of attempts to define religion (both in academic circles and public debates) are based on a list of concrete elements. They are sometimes called "substantivist definitions," because they try to describe the different core elements ("substances") inherent in every religion.

Wikipedia's definition — today's most globalized

encyclopedia — can be regarded as a particularly typical example in this regard. Here is the very first paragraph of the entry on religion:

> Religion is usually defined as a social-cultural system of designated behaviors and practices, morals, beliefs, worldviews, texts, sanctified places, prophecies, ethics, or organizations, that generally relates humanity to supernatural, transcendental, and spiritual elements; however, there is no scholarly consensus over what precisely constitutes a religion.[57]

At the core of this brief definition lies an interesting irony: although the second sentence says there is no consensus, the first sentence makes a firm attempt to define the concept. More specifically, the authors try to describe religion on the basis of a few discrete characteristics. The problem with such definitions, however, is that the majority of those concrete characteristics are often lacking in many belief systems and ways of life that are consistently labeled as religious. The three elements most frequently mentioned as core aspects of religion (and which are also included to a greater or lesser extent in this Wikipedia definition) have already been discussed in previous chapters: divine or transcendent elements do not always occupy a central role in the "social-cultural system" of religion; when taken as a whole these systems are not hierarchically structured; and they cannot always be neatly classified on the basis of their convictions or practices.

It goes without saying that other, even more specific elements that are sometimes mentioned in definitions are not always present either. For example, in various religions, there is no canon of holy texts containing prophecies, and community building is by no means essential since many traditions also know eremitic ascetics who completely isolate themselves from the world.

We simply cannot connect all religions from Islam to Jainism and from Taoism to Mormonism by checking off a list of characteristics. To circumvent that problem, some propose to approach these characteristics as a matter of "family resemblance." This would remove the necessity to check off every element of the list. It may suffice to find *several of the typical elements* in a particular tradition for it to qualify as a religion. In one tradition perhaps we do not find any belief in God, but we do encounter a form of cultic worship based on a holy scripture. In another tradition perhaps we do not find any scripture, but we do encounter a community which upholds certain ethical guidelines. This would still allow us to designate them as religions, even if certain characteristics are absent.

However, this idea of family resemblance makes it extremely difficult to distinguish between the secular and the religious. Take, for example, the investiture of a king. We generally do not consider this to be a religious event even though it contains a mixture of rituality, community building and hierarchy, which are all different characteristics that are often associated with the religious. Or take, for example, ecological activists who want to protect "Mother Earth" and therefore choose a strictly vegan lifestyle. This involves higher principles, a strong ethical worldview and explicit behavioral rules. Again, these are all elements that are invariably associated with religion. However, ecological activists will not be described as "adherents of a religion."

The crux of the problem should be obvious. If we make the definition narrow enough to be specific—for example, by stating that a sociocultural group must contain a belief in a creator God to count as religion—it no longer applies to many traditions that are considered to be religions today. On the other hand, if we make the definition broad enough to encompass a wide range of traditions—for example, by emphasizing the idea of family resemblance—it also encompasses many phenomena that are normally not considered to be religious.

Since substantivist definitions based on "lists" are inherently flawed, some academics suggest more functionalist definitions. These no longer define religion on the basis of *the content* of certain ideas and rituals, but on the basis of *the role* they play within a certain community and society. As such, it does not matter whether someone prays to a God or looks at the universe in a totally materialistic way. What matters is the sociopsychological function certain ideas and rituals fulfill. In concrete terms, this concerns proposals such as "religions give meaning to life" or "religions provide connection within one's own community, while simultaneously setting boundaries with other communities."

Although such functionalist definitions might, at first, seem to solve some definitional problems by abandoning the search for specific characteristics, ultimately, they are not far removed from the substantivist definitions. They only happen to focus on a different kind of characteristic. They do not concentrate on certain convictions, rules, or structures, but single out their function in society. As a result, we end up facing the same problems. If we define this function too narrowly, we can point to religious movements that do not fulfill it. If we define this function more broadly, it turns out that they apply equally well to secular phenomena.

Take, for example, the ritual significance of raising a flag or singing an anthem within the context of a highly nationalist state. Such rituals give meaning to the world by affirming the patriotism of some people, and it clearly provides both connection within one's own community and differentiation with other communities. Within the more common functionalist definitions, we could therefore simply label any form of nationalism as a religion.

Interestingly enough, some proponents of functionalist

definitions do not consider this to be a problem. On the contrary, they admit wholeheartedly that their definitions also apply to phenomena that are usually referred to as secular. What is more, they often will use functionalist definitions to demonstrate how diverse phenomena such as nationalism, the market economy, and consumerism, actually function as new forms of religion in the contemporary world. Yet, if all of these phenomena are also religious, it becomes even harder to determine what exactly the concept of "religion" entails—or at the very least, the distinction between the religious and the secular ceases to have any significance.

For several decades, these inherent definitional problems have been discussed extensively in important articles and books written by leading researchers.[58] Nevertheless, some academics maintain that we can still distinguish the religious from the secular. The reasoning often goes like this: "It may be difficult to strictly delineate the concept, but religion carries something within it that everyone eventually recognizes. We may not be able to define it properly, but we can point to a religious phenomenon when we see it." Differently put: we intuitively notice religion when we are exposed to it.

That may sound plausible to some, but all in all, it still fails. Today most people assume that religion is a fundamental aspect of all cultures and that it has therefore exerted a strong influence on traditional societies. If that is so and if the category of religion is truly self-evident on an intuitive level, we might assume that classical stories and foundational texts of every community regularly refer to religion (or an equivalent term) and indicate which place it should or should not be given within society. Yet, as it turns out, this is not the case. Most belief systems and ways of living that we nowadays designate as "religions" did not previously define themselves that way. Ancient Chinese who read the classics of Taoist teachings, medieval Hindus

71

who listened to the preaching of their guru, or North American indigenous tribes who told ancient traditional stories during an annual ritual, would not have come across the concept of "religion." It simply was not a distinct theme in their cultural context. Their languages did not even have a word for it.[59]

As important as the concept of "religion" might be in our contemporary globalized world, it is not an age-old and universal concept. It is specifically linked to the context and history of Western Europe. It makes sense, therefore, to dig a little deeper into the fascinating origin and evolution of the word.

On the origin and evolution of "religion" as a concept

From ritual practices to matters of faith

People who inquire about the etymology of the word "religion" are often told it comes from the Latin *religare*, "to bind something together (again)." As such, it would be possible to read two meanings in the root of the word: connecting people in a (faith) community and/or connecting an individual with God. However, there is also another possibility, which was once suggested by the well-known Roman statesman Cicero. He proposed that the word *religio* came from *relegere*, which carried meanings such as "to reread," "to study thoroughly" and "to consider deeply." In that respect, it would rather refer to "handling something carefully," as a sort of antithesis to the word *neglegere*, that is to say, "handling something carelessly." This would in fact make a lot of sense since the word *religio*, in everyday conversation among ancient Romans, mainly designated careful, correct, and proper comportment. Consequently, when Romans spoke of "religions" in plural, they were not talking about different sets of belief systems but were instead referring to the specific rituals to be performed in the temples.

> ## Christians without "religio"
> In the Roman Empire *religio* was more a matter of orthopraxy than orthodoxy. That is why some Roman authors wrote in their polemical tracts that Christians were to be distrusted because they had *no religio at all*. However, this did not imply that the early Christians did not uphold any specific belief system. Being blamed for not having any *religio* meant that they could not rely on a longstanding tradition. Consequently, they were despised for refusing to uphold the social customs of the past. After all, upholding the ancient rituals was seen as an important binding factor of society. In other words, the problem was not so much that Christians believed in a different God, but rather that they did not respect traditional customs and that they were therefore subversive.[60]

As such, in the early centuries of Christianity, religion was not an important concept. Very few books were devoted to the theme. Moreover, since the word "religion" originally referred to ritual practices, it was mainly connected with a monastic lifestyle. In the Middle Ages then, it was predominantly used to denote a distinction between the "religious" and "secular" branches of the Catholic Church. "Secular" did not refer to the contemporary idea, however. Rather, it referred to the well-known line of pope, bishops, priests, deacons, and laity, who lived and worked "in the world" and was thus contrasted to the "religious" line of the Church, which consisted of those who lived according to a monastic rule with its many daily rituals.

Nevertheless, during the Middle Ages, a slight shift in the meaning of the word also occurred. Some started to approach religion as one of the minor virtues, alongside the more important virtues such as faith, hope, and love. We can see this, for example, in the texts of Thomas Aquinas, who is one of the most influential theologians in the history of Catholicism.

He describes religion as the virtue that causes one to focus inwardly on God when performing certain actions. Yet, even in this particular instance, the word "religion" remained closely associated with ritual customs. For, in accordance with the medieval worldview in which body and mind formed an intricate whole, such a virtue had to be manifested in concrete actions. Accordingly, Aquinas thought that the monastic life was the most eminent example of the virtue "religion." After all, monks were supposed to discipline both body and soul to dedicate their entire lives to God.

Consequently, people were still a long way from the contemporary concept of religion near the end of the Middle Ages. In some respects, we may see some similarities, such as an emphasis on ritual, an inner focus on God, and monastic life as an explicit example of religion. But we mainly see important differences. It is *not* about a set of beliefs. It is *not* a separate dimension of society of which we can see different variations in all cultures. And it is *certainly not* a sociocultural phenomenon that we can oppose to the present-day concept of "secularity."

It was only from the Protestant Reformation onwards that religion was gradually seen as a separate dimension of society. Protestants were vehemently opposed to the Catholic Church teachings which instructed people to earn their way to heaven through all kinds of deeds and rituals. Protestant preachers instead emphasized the notion that "only faith saves." Consequently, when they used the word "religion," they increasingly emphasized its inner dimension. This inner impulse was the most prominent facet of faith, not because it encouraged people to engage in the correct method of (ritual) worship of God, but because the inner impulse toward faith in God was, *in itself,* the ultimate expression of that faith. Owing to this, practice became secondary, and religion primarily became a matter of belief.

This conceptual move eventually also made it possible to separate "the religious" from "the secular" because if religion is understood as solely revolving around inner beliefs and motivations, it can subsequently be distinguished from outer actions and contexts. As a result, over the course of the sixteenth century, we can see a shift in the meaning of the word toward the dichotomy that still forms the basis of our contemporary understanding of religion: a distinction between an internal dimension (convictions, faith, religious experience) and an external dimension (ritual, structure, community). It is a distinction between a domain for "faith and God" and a domain for "the world." A distinction, therefore, between a religious dimension and a secular dimension.

However, that shift in meaning did not happen in a vacuum. It was closely intertwined with the political context of the time, which was strongly influenced by the rise of the nation-state, to which I will now turn.

Religion and the rise of nation-states

As the political elites of the new European nation-states sought ways to legitimize their power against the power of the Catholic Church, they had every interest in exclusively linking religion to inner beliefs. Not only would this allow them to sharply delineate the domain of the church ("the religious") from their own ("the secular"), but it additionally allowed them to make one subordinate to the other: religious convictions are supposed to be kept private, while the law of the state applies within the public sphere.

This "privatization" of religion also involved another important shift in meaning. It became possible to formulate religion as an abstract concept of which there are various external expressions and forms. Thus, the idea of religions as a multiplicity was born: different belief systems that have a similar goal, but pursue this goal in fundamentally different ways.

In this way, it might seem that the contemporary concept of religion had fully formed. However, that was not the case just yet. When the plural "religions" was used, it initially indicated the various Christian divisions, and the singular "religion" was still associated with Christian truth. There were only different possibilities to interpret this truth and shape it into reality. In this regard, we nowadays would rather speak of "Christian denominations" and not of individual religions.

In some works, written by humanists and Enlightenment thinkers, we can already find some hints toward considering Islamic and Jewish traditions as "religions" as well. However, terms such as "Buddhism," "Sikhism," or "Shintoism" were far from being included at that time.[61] To achieve this, the meaning of the word "religion" needed to undergo one final shift, which only took place in the nineteenth century as part of broader colonization processes.

Colonialism and the further development of "religion" as a concept

Before the European colonization period, the cultural diversity of the world was not classified by demarcating the different religions. Rather, Europeans divided the world into four population groups, which were often designated as "nations." As such, they spoke of the Christian nation, the nation of the Mohammedans, the nation of the Jews, and the nation of the heathens. The latter were also regularly referred to as idolaters, polytheists, or pagans.

Jews and Mohammedans were, in many respects, viewed in a negative and hostile manner, but they were still believed to worship the one true God. Since the heathens and polytheists supposedly did not, their way of life was deemed to be insignificant. Wherever they lived and whatever their traditions, rituals, or beliefs, they were lumped together in the same category. What is more, the sheer diversity of customs and practices within that group was taken as proof of the fact that they had obviously deviated from the pursual of the one true

God—and therefore had *no* religion!

> ## Cultures without religion
>
> It sounds rather absurd to us today, but the records of colonial scouting missions (usually more romantically referred to as "the explorations of the age of discovery") regularly indicated that they had found no trace of religion among the people they encountered. Professor William Cavanaugh once summed up a couple of examples in his book *The Myth of Religious Violence*: "Amerigo Vespucci remarked on the lack of religion" among the Caribbean peoples he encountered. Sixteenth-century conquistador Pedro Cieza de León found the Peruvians "observing no religion at all, as we understand it." The seventeenth-century explorer Jacques Le Maire found in the Pacific islands "not the least spark of religion," and the eighteenth-century trader William Smith reported that Africans "trouble themselves about no religion at all."[62]
> Early missionaries who were active in India also sometimes indicated in their letters that they had not seen religion anywhere and the South African Khoikhoi were not initially thought of as having a religion either.[63]
> Cavanaugh summarizes the political and ideological cause behind this "blindness" as follows: "In their initial encounters, Europeans' denying religion to indigenous peoples was a way of denying them rights. If they lacked a basic human characteristic like religion, then native peoples could be treated as subhumans without legitimate claim to life, land, and other resources in their possession. Once the native peoples were conquered and colonized, however, it was 'discovered' that they did in fact have religions after all, which were then fitted into [their own and newly developed] taxonomies of religion."[64]

In the course of the eighteenth and nineteenth centuries, however, the perspectives on humanity drastically changed. European imperialist powers occupied ever more territory and expanded their colonization. An urge to "discover" as much as possible made them collect ever more information about the cultures and societies they encountered but were not well acquainted with. On the one hand, this was the result of the growing faith in "science" and the accompanying need to categorize everything according to modernist and rationalist frameworks. On the other hand, it was hoped that acquiring knowledge would help to exert greater control over colonized societies.

This attempt to gain more information also meant that some people wanted to map the religious diversity of the colonies. However, they mainly did so from a Christian perspective. They looked for "beliefs" (by analogy with the creeds and dogmas of Christianity); they looked for priestly hierarchies (by analogy with the ecclesiastical structures in Christianity); and they looked for conflicts between religious groups (by analogy with the tensions between Catholics and Protestants). As such, Western intellectuals certainly did not always make thorough efforts to comprehend the different traditions from within their own contexts. Rather, they projected their own cultural and religious concepts onto the diverse communities they explored in attempts to catalog them within their own worldview.

The colonial context thus brought about another transformation in the meaning of the word "religion." After all, the concept had now been disconnected from its Christian context. It was no longer necessary to view religion as a matter of belief in God as the one almighty creator. Polytheists, as well as those who did not believe in a transcendent concept of God, could now be regarded as religious, and their respective traditions could therefore be described as separate religions (while the different branches of Christianity were no longer described as separate religions, but became different denominations of the same religion). Since then, religion is not only a concept that is based on belief and faith, that comes in different variants, and that is distinguishable from the secular dimensions of society; it also became a dimension of existence that, *by definition,* can be found in *all* cultures.

Understandings of religion from the twentieth century onwards

This novel view on religion led to an increasing division of the whole of humanity into different religious communities. With all kinds of historical, anthropological, sociological, theological, and linguistic research, an attempt was made to achieve an overview of the enormous variation that existed in the field. However, academics discovered such a wide range of religious beliefs, practices, rituals, and ways of life, that by the early twentieth century they were confronted with the question posed at the beginning of this interlude: if the differences are so abundant, what then is the common thread?

Several attempts were made to answer that question but, for the reasons already explained, none of those answers sufficed. From the middle of the twentieth century onwards, academic researchers began to critically investigate the concept of "religion." They emphasized the definitional problem and made it clear that the concept might not be applicable to all cultures after all.[65]

Yet even though the group of anthropologists and religious scholars who argue for a radical rethinking (and sometimes even for an abolition) of the term "religion" gradually grew, they do not exert a strong influence on its contemporary usage. In other academic disciplines, in political debates, and in media reporting, the mainstream view of religion is still based on seventeenth-, eighteenth-, and nineteenth-century ideology. As a result, religion is generally described as a phenomenon that is mainly based on strict beliefs and rules of conduct. On the one hand, it is assumed that there are many similarities between the different religions, such as the fact that they preach a belief in divine beings, or the fact that the followers of a religion have to accept the authority of a religious elite. On the other hand, it is presumed that there are also many important differences between separate religions which lead to conflicts between them. Mainly because of this inherent tendency toward dogmatic violence it is surmised that religion should remain a private matter whenever possible. From this perspective, religion can only be given space as an inner, personal, and spiritual experience that distances itself from more outward, well-defined, and all-too-strict notions of religiosity.

We can wrap up our historic overview here. However timeless the word "religion" may sound today, it turned out to be very contingent. As we have seen, it underwent significant shifts in meaning over the course of its history, and the different ways in which it has been interpreted during the past two millennia are closely intertwined with political upheavals in Europe. Exactly because of the latter, it remains a highly loaded concept.

For this same reason, it is of great importance that we conclude this interlude with a closer look at a particular sociopolitical element which is closely connected with all of this. While it may sound surprising to many, the way we eventually came to look at religion is also linked with overt racism. Only when we face this aspect can we truly understand the origin of the seven myths about religion and how they have been sustained into the contemporary age.

On the racist dimensions of conceptualizing "religion"

As I already mentioned, during the eighteenth and nineteenth centuries, Europeans increasingly assumed that the whole of humanity could be divided into different religions, whereas previously they used to speak of four overarching "nations." The urge to create a taxonomy of these religions in as much detail as possible was therefore quite intense. Moreover, the academic efforts in this regard, from the outset, were closely enmeshed with the politics of colonization and the ensuing power dynamics between colonizer and colonized. Probably no one summarized this more concisely than the nineteenth-century Max Müller, one of the most important philologists and scholars of comparative religion. He once wrote: "Let us take the old saying, *divide et impera*, and translate it somewhat freely by 'classify and conquer.'"[66]

Based on this attempt to "classify and conquer," the various religions were initially classified into "world religions" and "ethnic" (or "national") religions. The first group included those religions that had spread to larger parts of the world, and somehow contained an inherent, universalist perspective. The second group included all other religions that were only intended for a particular community and had difficulties crossing the borders of their native region due to their conceptual limitations.

Interestingly enough, it was the "discovery" of Buddhism that initially gave birth to the category of "world religions." Since more and more texts from the Buddhist canon were translated, and new information was unearthed about the figure of the Buddha, researchers noticed that the scriptural canon and the Buddha were very influential in multiple countries. Until then, however, Christianity was regarded as the only truly universal tradition. So, when academics in the nineteenth century noticed how widespread the Buddha's teachings were, they were faced with a problem: Christianity was no longer the only tradition that transcended regional borders. As such the category "world religions" came to the fore.[67]

This of course begs the question why Islam had not been designated as a world religion long before encountering various Buddhist communities. After all, Europeans had been confronted with Islam for several centuries and were well aware of its worldwide spread. For most academics, the answer to that conundrum was obvious: Islam was not a world religion, but clearly an ethnic religion that had transcended its "natural" boundaries. Building on age-old portrayals that dismissed Islam as Christianity's demonic enemy, Islam was thought of as "too barbaric" to be a true world religion. It was believed that the harsh, aggressive ideas of Islam, with which the Prophet Muhammad united various Arab tribes, was being imposed on others. As a result, it was argued that this religion ended up in cultural contexts where it was out of place.

Thus, in the nineteenth century, religions were not only categorized, but they were also hierarchically ordered. Christianity was seen as the most exalted religion, Buddhism was highly appreciated, Hinduism was sometimes dismissed as primitive idolatry while at other times perceived as an exotic curiosity, and Islam was, by definition, problematic, as was Judaism. Thus, the many religions were placed on a scale from "local and primitive" to "universal and rational."

This hierarchical interpretation of religions was reinforced by the contemporary academic developments in linguistics. During the nineteenth century, philologists discovered different language groups and attempted to relate them to the "inherent character" of their original communities and races. For example, the grammatical structure of Semitic languages such as Hebrew and Arabic was considered to be very base and narrow. This was seen as a reflection of the limited mental capacities of the people who spoke these languages. The racial character of Semitic people was portrayed as primitive, harsh, and incapable of detecting universal truths. Accordingly, Islam and Judaism were presented as religions that inherently want to impose their uncivilized laws and regulations on others by force.

This image was contrasted with the image of Aryan people,

such as the ancient Greeks, who were seen as the forerunners of the Europeans. Their Aryan languages were considered to have great flexibility because they supposedly reflected the more rational mind and civilized character of the Aryan races. So, if Christianity had eventually grown into a worldwide religion, the reasoning went, it was because it had outgrown its Semitic origins and absorbed the more rational, sophisticated Aryan thought. This allowed it to develop a truly universal message.

According to this theory, Indian traditions were also Aryan in origin, as they have a linguistic link with European languages. It was therefore believed that a sophisticated and universal message could also be found in the Vedas but that this message was obscured by the Brahmin priestly class and by gradual corruption because of popular superstitions.[68] Accordingly, many researchers saw the Buddha as a kind of Indian Luther who wanted to liberate the Hindus from their irrationality and their priestly classes. This offered an explanation as to why Buddhism had become a "world religion" and Hinduism had remained an "ethnic religion."

From the end of the nineteenth century onwards, however, the specific dichotomy of "world religions" versus "ethnic religions" disappeared. In the twentieth century, the hierarchical interpretation gradually gave way to a more pluralistic and egalitarian view among religious scholars, anthropologists, and historians. Although the term "world religions" was preserved, it took on a different meaning. Nowadays, it no longer refers to an inherent universalist tendency, or to the fact that a large number of adherents can be identified in different geographical areas. Rather, the term refers to a somewhat vague idea like "the larger religious traditions." In general, this encompasses a series of religions such as Christianity, Judaism, Islam, Hinduism, Jainism, Taoism, Shintoism, Buddhism, Confucianism and Sikhism. Sometimes certain traditions are left out of the list (because, for some reason, they are not considered to be a religion) and sometimes other traditions are added (such as Zoroastrianism or Baha'ism). During the twentieth century, the same "world religions" repeatedly cropped up in corresponding lists.

The concept of "national" or "ethnic" religions took a different turn. The terminology itself disappeared, but under the skin of the general discourse on religion—and not very deeply under that skin—its connotations were preserved. This becomes amply clear from the same lists of world religions, or rather, from the religious contexts those lists so frequently omit. In the instances where they are in fact mentioned, they are still referred to geographically or racially by descriptions such as "the traditional African religions," "the animism of Native American tribes" or "the spirituality of the Aboriginals." It is therefore striking that only Asian religions (such as Hinduism, Taoism or Shintoism) and God-oriented religions (such as Judaism, Islam, or Zoroastrianism) are mentioned. African, South American, and Oceanic traditions generally do not even get a separate name. In other words, we often do not even bother to label religions when we find them in regions so heavily Christianized through colonization efforts, that few traces of the old traditions are left (unless via syncretic admixtures with Christianity). The few elements of the older traditions that still survive are usually bundled together with container terms such as "shamanism" and "animism." Of course, this does not deviate very much from the pre-eighteenth-century custom of clustering all lesser-known traditions together indiscriminately as "heathendom" or "paganism."

In this respect, Jonathan Z. Smith, one of the leading figures of the academic research that critically examined the concept of "religion" at the end of the twentieth century, once commented:

It is impossible to escape the suspicion that a world religion is simply a religion like ours, and that it is, above all, a tradition that has achieved sufficient power and numbers to enter our history and form it, interact with it, or thwart it. We recognize both the unity within and the diversity among the world religions because they correspond to important geopolitical entities with which we must deal. All "primitives," by way of contrast, may be lumped together, as may the "minor religions," because they do not confront our history in any direct fashion. From the point of view of power, they are invisible.[69]

This being the case, then, the term "religion" certainly was not always used in a completely harmless manner. It is not just a neutral, descriptive word. On the contrary, behind the contemporary usage of the term lies a problematic colonial history.

This does not necessarily imply that the word "religion" is inherently racist and that we should therefore immediately remove it from our vocabulary. However, we do have to be aware of such historical elements since some of them still permeate the way in which the concept is typically interpreted today. Although the contemporary view of religion originally arose from within an explicitly Christian framework, the same ideas were eventually adopted by more atheistic and modernist frameworks. Christianity served as a yardstick for Christian colonials. All other religions were considered inferior in several respects. Christianity had triumphed all over the world because it supposedly was the one and only true religion. Yet, the contemporary modernist view of the world *also* sees its own context as a yardstick. All societies where religion still plays an important role are considered to be inferior to the more secularized societies. Secular, liberal democracies have triumphed all over the world because they supposedly offer the only rational approach. Christian triumphalism thus became secular triumphalism.

In the end, the only difference between the colonial Christian view of religion and the contemporary modernist view of religion, is the perception of Christianity. In the past, many believed that the shortcomings of other religions no longer applied to Christianity. Today, those shortcomings are thought to apply to religions in general. So, just as many Christians wished to spread Christianity around the world as the only true teaching, many today are convinced that the whole world must secularize, and that all people must be freed from their religious constraints.

In short, the distinction between "secular" and "religious" still maintains a distinction between superior and inferior. Whereas previously people thought in terms of "true believers" versus "pagans" and later construed a binary between "universal, rational religions" and "local, primitive religions," nowadays the dichotomy is one of "we, the enlightened" versus "they, the ones who are still a bit behind."

With this consideration, we come to a close of the interlude, which will inform a common thread running through the following chapters. Unlike the previous chapters, the proceeding ones will not investigate specific characteristics that are ascribed to religion, but rather engage with different dualities that are central to the modernist distinction between the secular and the religious: "we are spiritual and free, while they still cling to their religious attachments," "we are rational and modern, while they resist scientific knowledge," and "we have transcended religious violence, while they are still trapped in it." Echoes of these dualities can be heard in all sorts of contemporary discussions about religion. Yet, once again, numerous examples will make it amply clear how problematic these dualisms can be.

Myth #4

Spirituality and Mysticism Contrast with Religion

"I am spiritual, but not religious." Since the turn of the millennium this expression became increasingly commonplace. According to various surveys, more than a quarter of the population in the US and several European countries self-define as such.[70]

When you ask people why they describe themselves this way, you are generally presented with arguments that closely relate to the ideas about religion discussed in the first three chapters. A recurring theme appears of religion being a hierarchical entity that propagates dogmas and obliges adherence to strict rules. Consequently, "religion" is contrasted with terms such as "spirituality" and "mysticism" because the latter supposedly allows people to search for inner depth in a more personal manner and thus offer a possibility to create one's own image of God, while remaining open to the ideas of others.

So, even though many people have a feeling that spirituality is somehow connected with religion, they often assume that spirituality and mysticism are restricted by too much religiosity. *True* spirituality and mysticism (devoid of religion) are seen as individual and inner processes, which allow every person to freely experience a deeper part of reality. Consequently, the more spirituality and mysticism are manifested in public rituals, the more suspicion they arouse. As soon as spirituality becomes something external, it once again belongs to the realm of old-fashioned, dangerous religion that curtails one's personal growth.

However, this modern dichotomy between "religion" on the one hand and "mysticism and spirituality" on the other is difficult to substantiate. In fact, such a dichotomy does not make our contemporary spirituality more open or free. Rather, it makes our understanding of religion more confused. Looking at some concrete examples will, once again, aid in clarifying why this is the case. Take "Sufism," for instance: in both popular spiritual literature and academic reference works, the term designates a mystical branch of Islam with more spiritual tendencies, and which is therefore marginalized by mainstream Islam. Yet, mysticism and spirituality are not some oddities on the margins of Islam. On the contrary, as I will show in the following short exposition, they occupy a very central place.[71]

On the centrality of spirituality and mysticism in Islam

Contemporary geopolitical tensions are often construed as an opposition of "Islam" versus "the West," which strongly emphasizes the problem of Islamic fundamentalism. In this context, "Sufism" is often advanced as a sort of solution. It is presented as a separate, mystical form of Islam associated with poetry, music, and trance which falls somewhat outside "ordinary" Islam.

However, once we take a closer sociological, historical, anthropological, and theological look at the various expressions of Islamic mysticism, it becomes impossible to separate the religious parts from the spiritual and mystical. An obvious example is the life and work of Al-Ghazali, one of the greatest theologians in Islamic history. He was also a highly respected academic in his own day. Yet, because of a personal crisis, he abandoned his post and, for many years, walked the path of mysticism. However, these spiritual wanderings did not make him discard everything he previously taught. Instead, he absorbed his newfound mysticism *into* his theology and vice versa, allowing him to finally write his greatest work, the *Ihya' Ulum al-Din* (*The Revival of the Religious Sciences*), which, to this day, remains one of the most cited Islamic texts after the Qur'an and the classical hadith collections.

In the life of the well-known poet Rumi, spirituality and religion also cannot be separated. Rumi's poetry contains many beautiful verses on love and mystical union with the divine, making him very popular among Westerners otherwise unfamiliar with Islam. Since the end of the twentieth century American and European bookstores have sold a steady stream of translations and interpretations of his work. However, contrary to how it is often presented, Rumi's mystical love poetry did not just appear out of thin air. It was not some anomaly. His father, just as well, was an acclaimed mystic. Yet, his spiritual outlook did not prevent him from sending Rumi to Damascus to get classical training as a theologian and jurist.

The same problematic duality is prevalent in descriptions of Islam's structure since Sufi groups are often isolated from other segments such as the classical Sunni schools of law and the Shia movements. In reality, they have always been part and parcel of both. To cite just two examples: the Mevlevi (the famous "whirling dervishes") are Sunni Hanafites, and the Bektashi are a part of Shia Alevism.

Islamic mysticism is also omnipresent in the daily experience of Islam: Gnawa music in Morocco, Zar rituals in Egypt, Dhikr sessions in Chechnya, gatherings at mausoleums in Pakistan where hundreds of thousands of pilgrims are ecstatically dancing in the street. It is present everywhere.

As such, the mystical and spiritual verses of the Sufis are not a modern academic rediscovery of ancient wisdom which had somehow been lost. For centuries, those verses have been recited and sung by the average Pakistani, Iranian, and Turk. So, what we call "Sufism" today and consider to be "a separate, mystical branch of Islam" is not marginalized at all. Rather, in much of the Islamic world, it is the norm.

It is also important to recognize that the word "Sufism" is in fact a problematic translation of the Arabic word *tasawwuf*. In fact, it is rather peculiar to translate *tasawwuf* with an "-ism." *Tasawwuf* is not a word that refers to a separate denomination of Islam that one may or may not adhere to. Rather, it is a word that refers to the inner dimension of the religious tradition. In that sense, it does correspond quite well to what is today designated as spirituality and mysticism, but it cannot be distinguished from the religious elements surrounding it. *Tasawwuf* is an essential element of Islam. This is made very clear by the fact that, for many centuries, *tasawwuf* was an important part of university curricula in universities from Cairo to Delhi. As a subject, it offered students various insights about the inner workings of the human mind and soul and was taught alongside *hadith* (the sayings and actions of the Prophet), *tafsir* (exegesis) and *fikh* (jurisprudence).

However, it is also undeniable that the mystical experience of the Islamic faith, in its various forms, used to be more prominent than it is today. In some Islamic milieus one notices a strong resistance to such expressions of traditional spirituality. However, this resistance only emerged at the end of the nineteenth and early twentieth centuries, because the systematic denunciation of "Sufism" by certain Islamic groups was tied to the ideological tensions and political upheavals of the time. It would take too long to fully explain these ideological and political evolutions, so I will simply indicate that the end of the colonization period witnessed the rise of Islamic movements who wished to eject the colonial rule from their countries by purifying their Islam—that is to say, by rejecting everything they deemed to be unorthodox accretions. To mobilize Muslim civilians against the illegitimate rulers, they tried to reconnect with the sources of their tradition with the hope of rediscovering the strength their people had lost. In their anti-colonial efforts to restore the glory of their *religion*, many pioneers of these reform movements turned away from the *mystical* manifestations of Islam. They saw it as one of the major causes of the decline of the

Islamic world. From their perspective, the focus on mysticism encouraged passivity, spread superstition, and promoted blind obedience to problematic spiritual leaders.

In fact, the perspective of these groups was strongly influenced by the works of the nineteenth century Western Orientalists: European academics who tried to map the cultures, religions, and social structures of "the East" as extensively as possible— especially in the context of the colonial power dynamics of the time. According to the Orientalists, authentic Islam was based mainly on texts, laws, and doctrinal beliefs. They saw the free, non-hierarchical, and fluid expressions of "Sufism" as an abnormality and something separate from "authentic Islam."

It is also important that these orientalist views about Islam and "Sufism" were strongly predicated on the racial stereotyping of their time. In earlier centuries, Muslims were often presented as overly sensual, hedonistic, and decadent. They were contrasted with the supposed piety and frugality of devout Christians. In the nineteenth century this stereotype changed. One specific impetus for these changes was the academic development in linguistics, already referred to in the interlude. Muslims were increasingly presented as strongly Semitic. In keeping with their Semitic language, their racial character was seen as primitive, harsh, rule-oriented, and violent. This was contrasted with the Aryan languages and characters of more "flexible" minds of the Europeans. As a result, the Orientalists found it difficult to relate the open and free nature of "Sufism" to the supposed rigid essence of Islam. Professor Masuzawa Tomoko describes all of this very succinctly in her well-documented book *The Invention of World Religions*:

> In obvious correlation to the vilifying and condescending image of Semitic Islam, there surged among European scholars a renewed interest in so-called Islamic mysticism. Sufism was particularly valorized as a higher form of

Islam, Persian (or possibly Indian or neo-Platonic) in origin, therefore essentially Aryan in nature, hence exterior to what was deemed Islam proper.[72]

Thus, both Muslim modernists and orientalists made use of the same dichotomy, albeit with differing appreciations. Orientalists admired Sufism precisely because it was not an "authentic" form of Islam or a "real" religion. Some Muslim modernists, on the other hand, rejected Sufism for the very same reasons. The result of *both* tendencies was that this underlying dualistic view of Islam took hold in both the East and the West during the first half of the twentieth century.

Even though this view has become more widespread in the last hundred years, anyone who considers Islam in both its historical and cultural breadth cannot but conclude that the conceptual split of spirituality and religion is by no means self-evident. It does not offer us a useful analytical framework to juxtapose open, free, and inner spirituality with closed, regulated, and external religion. It does, however, perpetuate a politically and ideologically charged vision which continues to play a major role in public discourse. It is therefore not so surprising that a completely different picture emerges as soon as one stops looking at such phenomena through this ideological lens.

Some examples of spirituality and mysticism as a core element in other religions

Anyone exploring the religious diversity in the world will encounter different forms of profound spirituality. It might sometimes be a bit more prominent and sometimes a bit less, but it is a core element of every religion.

In many traditions of the Far East, such as Hinduism, Taoism or Buddhism, this is obvious. A search for personal spiritual liberation is a core feature of these religions—if not in the everyday life of every person, then at least in the classical teachings. These traditions can hardly be any *more* spiritual in the contemporary sense of the word, even though, as the previous chapters have already elucidated, they can also be described as religious.

> ## Vivekananda and Ramakrishna
> Two concrete figures who exemplify the impossibility of separating religion and spirituality within Hindu traditions are the renowned Vivekananda and his guru Ramakrishna. As I already mentioned in the discussion of the third myth, Vivekananda repeatedly expressed the belief that all religions are ultimately nothing but different paths to the same two-pronged spiritual goal of inner liberation and union with a universal source that transcends all words. At the same time, Vivekananda is one of the most important reformers of contemporary Hinduism. Like many others of the Indian religious elite, he wished to unite the exceptionally disparate Hindu traditions in a Brahmanical vision and drawing heavily on ancient Vedic texts. In contrast, Vivekananda's guru, Ramakrishna, was an important Bengali mystic who was somewhat less adamant about properly adhering to the guidelines of the various Hindu schools of thought. He often experienced visionary trances and was known for his eccentric habits. For example, he sometimes placed his wife at the center of traditional rituals that would normally be performed in front of a statue of the goddess Kali. Nevertheless, Ramakrishna was the official Brahmin priest of a Kali temple in Dakshineswar.

It might seem less obvious, but such spirituality can also be found at the core of traditions such as Judaism and Christianity. Here too, we find various expressions of profound mysticism.

A striking (and perhaps somewhat unexpected) example

from Judaism is the connection between the Kabbalah and the Hasidim. The Hasidim are known today as ultra-Orthodox Jews. The men are dressed in black, have curly sidelocks and wear a high black hat. The women wear dark clothes and a wig. Their distinctive appearance epitomizes Judaism in the minds of many people, even though they are estimated to make up only five percent of the worldwide Jewish community. Moreover, the community did not exist until the eighteenth century. Its founder was Yisroel ben Eliezer, who was credited with the name Baal Shem Tov, "the master of good fame." His teachings were based on the mystical and esoteric wisdom of the Kabbalah, and he placed great emphasis on the concept of *devekut*, the attempt to "remain glued" to the divine essence that permeates all existence. In other words, he urged his followers to have their souls cling to God throughout all their actions. As a result, Hasidic Judaism also developed ecstatic *niggunim* music, in which emotional exclamations and phrases from the Torah are sung in an improvised and repetitive manner as a form of prayer.[73]

For a last and very explicit example of mysticism from the Christian tradition, we can refer to Saint Bernard of Clairvaux. He founded the Cistercian monastic order and was one of the most influential figures of late medieval Catholic Christianity. He was one of the counselors to the ruling popes and is renowned for being an important clerical preacher who called on the public to join the Second Crusade. Yet, Saint Bernard is also famous for his exquisite mystical literature. He wrote a collection of sermons on the Song of Songs, in which he interpreted the entire Biblical book as a metaphorical image for the union between the soul and God. According to Bernard, the verses from the Song of Songs describe how the deep yearning of man is answered by God's overwhelming love. This collection of sermons greatly influenced the later Christian mystics. As such, we can see that elements labeled as "religious" today were equally present in the life of Bernard as those undoubtedly considered to be "spiritual" — and he certainly was not alone in this respect.

All of this makes it clear that at least the larger religious traditions are overrun by spiritual elements. The reverse is also true: phenomena labeled as "spiritual but not religious" often turn out to portray many elements that are generally designated as religious. A good example of this is contemporary bodily yoga, which has become a worldwide practice. This type of exercise is often seen as a technique that anyone can integrate into his or her own personal spirituality because it is no longer linked to a specific religious tradition. However, several historical facts shed a completely different light on this idea. So, I will delve into the matter a little more deeply.

Why contemporary postural yoga is not just spiritual, but also religious

Most people associate yoga primarily with stretching and breathing exercises. These are seen as a means to relax and restore the balance between mind and body. It is also generally assumed that yoga exercises are based on ancient Indian traditions. However, that is not the case since this particular form of postural yoga (often more specifically referred to as "hatha yoga") only emerged in the twentieth century.

Of course, the word "yoga" itself has deep roots in Indian religious thought. For centuries it was a crucial concept in the philosophical-spiritual quest for deepened consciousness (*samadhi*), transcending worldly dualities (*advaita*) and liberation from suffering (*moksha*). In that context, yoga generally referred to a spiritual union of one's soul with the primal source of the universe. It could also refer to the different methods for attaining that spiritual union and the accompanying state of inner liberation. For example, the Bhagavad Gita, a classic Hindu text, talks about *karma yoga, bhakti yoga* and *jnana yoga*.

The first type of yoga leads to union with the deepest divine reality through "pure action" (that is, by not being attached to the fruit of one's action), the second yoga does so through devotion (that is, by complete surrender to God) and the third yoga does so through wisdom (that is, by recognizing that there is no distinction between our own innermost being and the divine unity of the universe).[74]

In some scriptures, postures (*asanas*) are occasionally mentioned, but in general, they prescribe traditional forms of meditation in which one typically assumes a sitting position and controls one's breathing as a prerequisite for concentration, prayer, and contemplation.[75] So, what we think of as yoga today was by no means a standard element of the classical Hindu traditions.

The groups who *did* experiment with unusual physical postures, found themselves on the margins of society as they were consciously choosing to turn social norms upside down. Their physical rituals were not limited to stretching postures and could often become quite extreme. They also regularly engaged in additional practices such as walking around in heavy chains or smearing their bodies with cremation ash. Their contortions were therefore not aimed at "leading a healthy and balanced life," but rather, were associated with magical practices and an attempt to gain occult powers. Sometimes they were even used as a way to beg in the streets by performing tricks.

These figures were sometimes referred to as "hatha yogis" but were not always clearly distinguishable from Islamic fakirs. Some of them were highly respected for their profound asceticism, their mental control, and their spiritual charisma, but many were also looked down upon. In fact, toward the end of the nineteenth century it was the norm in elite Hindu circles to portray them as charlatans and as figures who prevented those in the West from learning "real yoga." After all, the Hindu elites wished to connect with the modernist rationalism of the

West and therefore mainly promoted a more metaphysical yoga based on the philosophical and spiritual principles from their scriptures.

So, when hatha yoga eventually did became popular in the twentieth century, this was not because the first Hindu teachers in the West propagated such exercises. Rather, it was largely the result of a Western focus on cultivation of the body, often referred to as "physical culture."

Long before the rise of gyms and aerobics classes, various forms of physical exercise were extremely popular, including German and Swedish gymnastics. In the nineteenth century and the first half of the twentieth century, this physical culture was such a widespread, global trend that it became an established part of the curricula in European and American schools. Due to its ascribed importance, it even culminated in the organization of the first modern Olympic Games in 1896.

Moreover, this physical culture was firmly embedded in the nationalist and racist ideas of the time. Encouraging youngsters to practice gymnastics in groups was aimed at preserving the strength of the people and endorsing discipline to ensure that their race did not degenerate or become "effeminate." This can be seen in the format of gymnastics: they involved many postures that required sustained muscular tension and were often practiced in groups with coordinated movements, much like military drills. Physical culture therefore served a dual purpose: strengthening moral character and ensuring people were always in perfect shape, able to defend their country when necessary. The former was not only a minor detail. It was of great importance since the whole endeavor was strongly associated with values such as masculinity, patriotism, fair play, and faith. In the UK people even incorporated "muscular Christianity" as a term for the prevailing views on a healthy mind in a healthy body. Pastors and priests would thus enthuse the youth to be devout and exercise. The well-known Young Men's Christian Association (YMCA), for example, strongly propagated physical culture.

Professor Mark Singleton's book *Yoga Body: The Origins of Modern Posture Practice* gives an excellent description of the worldwide dynamics of physical culture, as the phenomenon certainly was not restricted to Europe and North America. It took root in the colonies because of two reasons: first, through reinforcing the idea that colonizers were clearly superior because of their physical strength, and second, through the introduction of physical culture into the Indian education and military system. As a result, Indians also started incorporating physical exercises in their own daily routines:

> Colonial educators tended to present Hindu Indians as a weakling race who deserved to be dominated. The British physical culture regimes, however, were adopted by Indians and used as components of nationalist programs of regeneration and resistance to colonial rule. It is in this context that asana began to be combined with modern physical culture and reworked as an "indigenous" technique of man-building.[76]

Singleton describes various factors, processes, and experiments which are responsible for the slow revision of yoga as an "Indian physical culture," but the eventual result is undeniable: during the first half of the twentieth century an entirely new form of yoga with a strong bodily focus was developed.

The Sun Salutation

A striking example of these processes is the *Surya Namaskar*, the well-known Sun Salutation. This flowing sequence of movements was lightly inspired by an existing ritual performed only by Brahmin priests in temples dedicated to the sun god Surya. However, only a superficial resemblance to this original ritual remains.

In fact, today's *Surya Namaskar* was first conceived by figures such as Bhawanrao Shriniwasrao Pant Pratinidhi and Kolar Venkatesh Iyer. The former saw daily and frequent repetition of the *Surya Namaskar* as a way to increase physical strength, the latter considered it to be a very good warm-up before starting his bodybuilding routine.[77]

Owing to these circumstances, Indians could easily make a connection between the new impulse toward physical culture exercises and the postures of the old hatha yogis. The latter were reinterpreted as the traditional Hindu wisdom about physical health and mental strength that predated Western physical culture.

As a result of the desire to demonstrate the antiquity and superiority of yogic knowledge, some of the early advocates started digging deeper into their own traditions and were inspired by texts concerning breathing techniques (such as *pranayama*), subtle energy channels in the body (such as *nadis*), and psychospiritual concepts (such as *chakras*). Here too, there was an exchange with spiritualist tendencies that were, at the time, exerting a great influence in the Western world. For example, several progressive American Protestant movements propagated the idea that spiritual strength, physical health, and general fulfillment of life depended on a harmonious association with the cosmos. These somewhat disparate, but popular, spiritual movements, which are often referred to with the umbrella term "New Thought," had a strong influence on popular forms of gymnastics which were predominantly aimed at women, as a counterpart to the many forms of physical culture for men. These so-called "harmonial gymnastics" were less focused on strength, and more on developing physical elegance and mental balance, thus emphasizing stretching exercises, breathing techniques and relaxation.[78]

During this interplay of "supply and demand" in segments of physical culture, as well as in spiritual circles from both India and the West, the nationalist and anti-colonial elements increasingly faded into the background. The patriarchal goal of making the nation and its citizens physically strong was omitted. An ever stronger emphasis was then placed on relaxation and natural healing, and the exercises became increasingly linked with spiritual and mystical ideas. Consequently, this interpretation of yoga seamlessly connected with hippie exoticism, New Age spirituality, and the new fitness fashions of the second half of the twentieth century. Thus, yoga gradually grew into the meditative health practice it is associated with today.

So, the yoga practiced in fitness clubs or dance halls since the beginning of the twenty-first century has little to do with the original concept of yoga. The wider religious framework has been abandoned and everything seems to be reduced to a series of physical exercises. It even bears little resemblance to the subversive practices of the earlier hatha yogis, who sometimes placed their bodies in similar positions. Contemporary yoga is more a gentle form of aerobics with an added layer of popular spirituality about "connecting with your inner self," "listening to your body" and "living from the heart."

Today's postural yoga could therefore be considered an example of the way in which people can be spiritual but not religious. Age-old spiritual concepts have been divorced from their original Hindu context and placed within a framework of personal development.

Yet, such an interpretation is not self-evident. Even though there is a clear break between these new forms of yoga and its earlier interpretations, and even though these novel forms are strongly influenced by the physical culture of the nineteenth and twentieth centuries, strong connections with the religious framework of the Hindu traditions remain. For example, a yoga course which teaches that the right breathing exercise can let our *prana* (life energy) flow and open our *chakras* (spiritual energy nodes) does in fact connect with old concepts from Hindu classics.

We should also not lose sight of the fact that these new yoga forms were developed by Hindus. They were, of course, influenced by the social dynamics of their time, but they were also inspired by their own cultural and religious context. That is exactly why it resonated with others who picked up the practice. As such, it is certainly not the case that contemporary yoga has become a purely Western concept. We can find yoga courses all over India, and several religious leaders integrate yoga exercises into their teachings. While it may not have been part of Hindu traditions in this specific form before, it certainly is today. In that respect, yoga is a good example of the fact that a religious tradition never stops evolving and accumulating, as was explained in Chapter 2.

Moreover, for many Western yoga practitioners, it is not simply a casual hobby. It offers them much more than a weekly opportunity to get away from the hustle and bustle of life. Some immerse themselves in Hindu traditions, recite classical mantras, and regularly visit their guru in India. Such an intense involvement with a tradition would normally be labeled as religious. So, where exactly can we draw the line? How many elements does one need to integrate into one's life to cease being purely spiritual and become religious after all? Is someone only considered to be a religious Hindu when they read the Vedas every day and uphold a strict vegetarian diet? As clarified in the first chapter, that would mean that a large proportion of Hindus would no longer be classified as such. Or can we label someone a Hindu as soon as they perform the Sun Salutation and use the *om* sound as a mantra in their meditation? If so, this would include a large group of people who mainly practice yoga as a relaxation method.

Such questions become even more difficult to answer if

we consider once again that religions can also be adhered to in predominantly orthoprax manners, making the beliefs of adherents of secondary importance. As mentioned in the second chapter, this is often the case among Hindus, but why then is practicing yoga in a fitness center not a sign of religiosity, even if the yoga practitioner does not hold any Hindu beliefs? After all, when an Indian practices yoga at home, it is quickly seen as an expression of his (orthoprax) religion, even if he does not hold any grand ideological views. So, we easily slip into a problematic and unfounded dichotomy: an Indian who practices yoga is religious, but a Westerner who practices yoga is spiritual. In other words, once again a racist element emerges: "they" are still religious (and therefore lag behind), "we" are only spiritual (and therefore more advanced)—even if there is essentially no difference at all.

As such, contemporary yoga is not an example of a phenomenon which can clearly be categorized as "spiritual but not religious." In fact, we can get a better grasp of the phenomenon if we see it as the result of various processes of religious syncretism. First, there was a syncretic movement in which nationalistic and Christian colonial elements were incorporated into Hindu contexts until a new type of yoga emerged which focused on postures. Then, there was a syncretic movement in which this new ritual practice was absorbed into Western spiritual circles. Eventually, the original concept took on a whole new meaning as an "ancient spiritual-energetic wisdom" and was spread all over the world. A concept that originated within a broader Hindu tradition was thus injected into the Western spirituality of self-fulfillment and vice versa.

I am certainly not trying to diminish the value of contemporary postural yoga by discussing all of these dynamics. Whatever their historical background might be, regular exercises and thorough breathing techniques are generally very beneficial for the majority of the population. I am simply trying to explicate that such modern practices are undeniably rooted in religious elements from various traditions and that they still portray an abundance of characteristics that are normally associated with religion. As such, it eventually seems impossible to classify them as "solely spiritual."

We could make similar analyses of other popular practices and phenomena since the extensive attempt to separate spirituality and religion has had a global impact. On the one hand, it allows specific parts of various traditions to be commercialized. On the other hand, it gives rise to the demonization of religions by first "extracting" their spiritual elements and subsequently contrasting those with the more ritual and doctrinal elements of that religion.

So, if we want to get a clearer picture of religion's place within society, it is also necessary to develop a deeper understanding of the relationship between religion and spirituality.

A different look at the relationship between religion and spirituality

The word "spirituality" is derived from the Latin *spiritus* ("spirit"). For some, the word evokes images of occult and unembodied beings outside of ourselves, while others associate it more with internal and profound experiences. In either case, it refers to the nonmaterial dimensions of existence. So, when we are dealing with the spiritual, we are focusing on something that we cannot perceive through our sensory organs.

In that regard, spirituality is quite simply an inherent part of religion. Chapter 1 revealed how religions are not just a matter of beliefs and rules of conduct. Experience and beauty are also of great importance, and these dimensions predominantly belong to the domain of spirituality. However, someone who gives them their proper due does not necessarily have to discard every doctrine or prescription from the related religion. Conversely, adopting certain traditional convictions or guidelines does not, by definition, make spirituality disappear.

Moreover, many prophets, saints and respected religious figures ridiculed formalistic behavior *precisely because* spirituality was the inner essence of their tradition. *Precisely because* mystical union with the divine was the ultimate goal of their religious beliefs, they opposed approaching religion as a rigid set of obligations. Yet, the opposite—a vague interiority without any form or stability—was denounced just as quickly by many spiritual masters. The eminent American-Iranian professor Hossein Nasr once described how an Iranian scholar, who had been one of his teachers of Islamic mysticism, presented him with an analogy in this regard:

> One day he said, "It is fine to be open-minded. To be open-minded is like having the windows of the mind open. It is like opening up the windows of a house. Now it is wonderful to open the windows of your house provided your house has walls. But if there are no walls, say, just two windows in the middle of the desert, it does not matter whether you close them or open them."[79]

Every religious tradition has an outer pole as well as an inner pole. The outer pole consists of rituals, structures, texts, moral codes, and symbols that bind a community together, while the inner pole consists of experience, reflection, consciousness, and contemplation that connect with a deeper reality. As a result, in various traditions we come across reflections about this bipolarity and the search for its proper balance.

This concept has seldom been worked out so thoroughly as in the twentieth-century perennialist philosophy of the Traditionalist School—of which the aforementioned Hossein Nasr was an important proponent. This body of thought had great influence, not only in academic circles and certain traditional religious groups, but also in many New Age circles.[80] A central element of Perennialism is the idea that, underlying all reality, there is an eternally present Truth that finds its own expression within every religious tradition. The way in which a religion focuses on that eternal, transcendent Truth is called "the esoteric," and the way in which a religion expresses that truth in concrete doctrines, stories, rites, and behaviors is called "the exoteric."[81]

However, when these perennialists spoke of the underlying esoteric truth of religions, they did not propose that all religions are essentially the same and that we can strip away all the exoteric religious elements until we are left with nothing but the spiritual, esoteric core. From their perspective, it is impossible to ignore the outward form of the various traditions. Religions can only pass on the deeper realities discovered by the great teachers if they *also* provide a concrete path that enables others to (re)discover those same deeper realities. As such the inner spiritual essence can never remain without an external form.

The Traditionalist School thus acknowledged and appreciated the differences between the various traditions. To them, the fact that various religions might lead to a spiritual essence that ultimately cannot be captured in one particular form did not mean that they are completely interchangeable. Rather, the various religions develop unique constellations, each of which approaches certain facets of the spiritual essence from its own (psycho)logic.

Returning to the metaphor of Chapter 3, we can perhaps phrase it this way: each "religious language" uses its own "words" and "grammar" to express a spiritual message. Although their words and grammar (of symbols, stories, rituals, and so on) will always fall short of fully conveying the message, without those religious words and grammar we cannot clarify any aspect of the message—just as we would not be able to communicate without language.

Spirituality and ritual, the esoteric and the exoteric, are thus inextricably linked. Together they form religion. Even if a particular religious community is extremely orthoprax and focuses almost exclusively on the correct implementation of certain precepts, there is still a spiritual esotericism beneath the exoteric nature of that orthopraxy. For example, when some people perform a ritual "simply because that is the way in which we do things" and not because some element of faith prompts them to do so, it often still denotes an attempt to connect with ancestors or to express a sense of community.

Similarly, pure esotericism also does not exist. There will always be an exoteric side. Even communities that boast about their lack of religious commandments always display a certain formality. Whoever has an honest look at the group dynamics of communities who suggest that their members are spiritual but not religious, will see that a student-master relationship often plays a central role; that certain relationships between members of the group determine its internal dynamics; that there is a specific atmosphere at meetings; and that they gradually develop their own rituals.[82]

Humans are part of the physical and relational world. What moves us on the inside finds expression in our bodies, languages and art forms. In other words: spirituality, by definition, "externalizes" and never remains "inner." As a result, every spirituality has its limitations and is never "completely free." Yet, at the same time, we are not limited to the outer pole of religion when we are rooted in a particular religious tradition. On the contrary, the different traditions each offer a range of concrete possibilities for discovering the inner pole.

This is by no means an innovative idea. As I already mentioned, it has been expressed by many sages from several different traditions. However, when we lose sight of this simple idea, our view of religion becomes distorted and we can no longer make sense of anyone's spirituality.

Science and Religion Are at Odds with Each Other

Whether in televised panel debates or in conversations among friends, discussions about the value and validity of religion often end up in a conceptual framework which pits religion against science. After all, in the eyes of many people, science represents a rational, factual view of the world, and religion pertains to irrational beliefs.

If we want to unpack this duality a little further in order to discern whether or not this view has any merit, we should first clarify what we exactly mean when using the word "science." Broadly speaking, the word can refer to two different things. In its strictest sense, it designates the scientific method: formulating falsifiable hypotheses, carrying out controlled empirical experiments, calculating the statistical validity of the results, formulating new hypotheses, and so on. In a wider sense, the word "science" hints at a general, critical, inquisitive attitude that measures and maps reality from a materialist perspective.

In the first interpretation of the word, a comparison between religion and science does not seem to be appropriate, because when science is delineated as "the scientific method," we end up comparing apples to oranges. The scientific method and religion are utterly different phenomena, each with its own goal and approach since religion is a broad sociological concept, while the scientific method is limited to a research technique. From that perspective, juxtaposing science and religion seems as nonsensical as comparing science and sports or pitting science against art.

The second interpretation is different. If science entails a particular way of looking at and interacting with the world, then it does indeed end up in the same territory as religion. However, ending up in the same territory does not necessarily imply competition or conflict. After all, as was already made clear in the first chapter, religion is not always based on dogmatic faith and, furthermore, every larger tradition can lay claim to a whole series of critical freethinkers.

If we browse through the history of the various religious traditions, we will also find that a dichotomy of science (as the search for rational facts) versus religion (as the domain of irrational belief) was rarely applicable. To clarify this, let us take a quick look at the historical relationship between science and religion in Christianity, because the so-called "conflict thesis" originally arose in a Christian context.

On the fact that Christianity and science can easily coexist—and why we are convinced otherwise

It often surprises people to learn that the medieval Catholic Church championed rational research and that Christian beliefs formed the basis of modern science. Nevertheless, one can easily read about such matters in several contemporary authoritative books on the history of science.[83]

The underlying motive of the Christian focus on research was pretty straightforward: since God created nature and did not act erratically and inconsistently, certain laws can be discerned within His creation. Consequently, by getting to know more about these laws of nature, Christians hoped to learn more about the Creator Himself. In this respect, several old Christian treatises—even those of some Church Fathers from the early centuries of Christianity—speak of "the book of nature." One could not only discover God through the Bible, but also through examining natural phenomena. It was therefore quite normal for medieval Christian intellectuals to "read" a combination of both the Bible and natural phenomena when trying to examine the place of humankind in the world and universe.

As a result, it is simply not the case that the Catholic Church (or the Christian faith in general) opposed scientific developments, or that every researcher who posited a novel idea was discredited by Church authorities. This challenges widely held ideas in today's perceptions of Christianity, but the historical facts show that the Church never endorsed the idea that the earth was flat, never forbade the anatomical dissection of human bodies, and never banned the number zero. In contrast, it did in fact actively support a variety of scientific research.

The history surrounding the slow acceptance of heliocentrism in Christian Europe is very telling in this regard. Although some people proposed that the earth revolved around the sun as soon as the early sixteenth century (usually based on the spiritual idea that the sun is more akin to the essence of God and therefore must be more central to the universe), the common conviction among astronomers and theologians alike was that the sun revolved around the earth. As such, when Copernicus propagated his ideas, they did not just appear out of nowhere. However, they did go against the prevailing beliefs of the intellectual elite—and thus, also went against official Church teachings. As it turns out, that was not a huge issue at the time. The controversy surrounding the proposal to place the sun at the center of our solar system for mathematical and physical reasons did not really take off until a few decades after the publication of Copernicus' well-known book *De revolutionibus orbium coelestium* (*On the Revolutions of the Celestial Spheres*).

Even more so, when ecclesiastical authorities finally started attacking his heliocentrism, they did not do so with fierce theological damnations. Their arguments were predominantly based on the scientific consensus of the time. When Copernicus' book made it onto the *Index librorum prohibitorum* (*the List of Prohibited Books*), it was only a temporary ban. A couple of corrections were ordered to clarify that heliocentrism was still only a hypothesis and not an established truth (which actually made sense, given that the evidence for the theory was, at this point in time, still insufficient). After these adjustments were added as additional notes, the book could once again be freely read. Moreover, when the Catholic Church implemented a calendar reform at the end of the sixteenth century, it was based on the astronomical tables of Copernicus. After all, these turned out to be much more accurate than the tables previously in use.

> ## Copernicus' religious beliefs
> In the history of the development of heliocentrism, it is also important to note that Copernicus was in no way "anti-religious." He dedicated his book to Pope Paul III and stated plainly that God is "the best and most orderly workman of all."[84] Precisely because of the latter, he could not reconcile himself with the calculation systems that were in use at the time. In his view, they were too cumbersome and disordered to explicate God's creation. Copernicus' attempt to devise a new cosmological system thus stemmed from a distinctly religious motivation.

In fact, heliocentrism only became a heated issue when the famous Galileo became involved. Contrary to popular belief, he also was not tortured or burned. For a long time, he even had a good relationship with the Pope Urban VIII. Nevertheless, because of the controversy generated owing to one of his books (which was partly due to a falling-out between him and that same Pope), he was eventually brought to trial. As a result, he found himself under house arrest. While thus detained, Galileo produced his *Discourses and Mathematical Demonstrations Relating to Two New Sciences*. This book, which made him one of the greatest scientists of all time in the eyes of future generations, was published surreptitiously, but was never placed on the list of prohibited books. There is also no evidence that the Church authorities harassed him any further. In the end, Galileo died peacefully and at an old age on the night of January 8, 1642.[85]

However, when we bring up such historical examples (and refute the common perceptions that surround them), it is of great importance to bear in mind that it is actually very difficult to analyze them properly using concepts such as "religion" and "science." In the interlude I already explained in detail how our contemporary interpretation of religion did not exist in antiquity and the Middle Ages, but only gradually took shape from the sixteenth century onwards. The same goes for the concept of "science." There certainly was no talk of a dichotomy between the two concepts in the time of Copernicus and Galileo. Just like the word *religio*, the word *scientia*, its Latin forerunner, underwent several changes in meaning. Only in the nineteenth century would it truly develop into the contemporary concept designating not only a specific method, but also invoking an aggregate of all academic research or sometimes even a general, rationalistic view of the world.

In fact, the semantic shifts that the word *scientia* underwent reveal interesting parallels with the semantic shifts surrounding the word *religio*. To start with, *scientia* initially did not refer to a dimension of society either. Rather, the word referred to a kind of skill and attitude, which anyone could develop as a personality trait. For example, someone like Thomas Aquinas called *scientia* an "intellectual virtue." He saw it as the inner capacity to demonstrate a certain truth through logical reasoning and argument. Those who mastered this virtue could apply it to various domains, such as grammar, mathematics, astronomy, music, geometry, and the study of nature. Whoever had made a habit of this *scientia* could thus also make use of it in the most important domain of all: theology and the search for divine truths.

Like many other scholars of his time, Thomas Aquinas thus placed himself in a long tradition that can be traced to figures such as Aristotle. After all, the philosophy of the ancient Greeks was not just a matter of inventing interesting ideas about the world and our place in it. Their efforts at acquiring knowledge (and developing ways of reasoning that could lead to that knowledge) were always embedded in the more general goal of cultivating a profound lifestyle, becoming a moral person, and discovering spiritual wisdom. The medieval Christian concept was very similar in these aims. Rational inquiry and logic were seen as part of the moral and spiritual development of the human soul.

The "scientific" approach of the ancient Greeks

The moral and spiritual focus of ancient Greek philosophy also sheds new light on the polemics of the early Christians. It is sometimes assumed that the early Christians rebelled against the scientific approach of the ancient Greeks owing to their novel religious beliefs. However, this is a profound distortion of the actual debates of those days. In fact, Christians distanced themselves from Greek philosophy because they viewed themselves as upholding a similar—but better—spiritual practice. For example, according to Professor Peter Harrison, someone like Saint Augustine claimed that "natural philosophy, moral philosophy, and logic were all contained in Christ's commandment to 'love God and your neighbor'—a claim that would seem far-fetched without the moral thrust of Pagan philosophy."[86]

In that regard, we can also reassess the common idea that the historical roots of modern, scientific thought can be traced to the Greek philosophers, which based themselves on a highly rational approach. It is often assumed that this "Greek spirit" was eventually rediscovered by the Enlightenment philosophers, allowing it to, once again, break free from the limitations of religion and finally shine its glory all over the world. However, according to

Professor Harrison this story is difficult to maintain:

"Comforting though this narrative may be for some, the reality is rather different. If we focus for now simply on the role ascribed to Greek science, we can say that its putative rejection of myth and supposed incompatibility with religion break down under close scrutiny. No one who has read the extant fragments of the pre-Socratic philosophers can fail to be struck by their ubiquitous references to gods and divine principles. Thales, the purported progenitor of science, declared that 'all things are full of gods,' and on discovering his famous theorem he is said to have sacrificed an ox. These are not the actions of a hard-nosed scientific naturalist. Anaxagoras (b. ca. 500 BC), like Thales, is often portrayed as exemplifying a scientific naturalism that is essentially incompatible with a theological understanding of the cosmos. This characterization draws some credibility from the claim that Anaxagoras was banished from Athens on account of his skeptical claims that the sun was just a mass of molten metal, that the moon was made of an earthlike substance, and that the stars were merely fiery stones. But it was this same Anaxagoras who contended that the whole universe was controlled by a divine causal principle (nous—mind or intellect), a view that was to influence, in various ways, Plato, Aristotle, the Stoics, and the Neoplatonists, and which came to underpin much of the subsequent ancient Greek belief in the inherent rationality of the natural world."[87]

Thus, the ancient Greek philosophers were no more "scientific" than those who came before or after them. Their rationality was equally intertwined with their

> religion: "Myths were not thought to offer alternative explanatory accounts to 'science.' Not only were they regarded as compatible with rational, philosophical accounts of the natural world, but they were also considered to be important vehicles for the transmission of profound philosophical truths."[88]

Only in early modern times would the view of *scientia* eventually change. However, this is not because the word *scientia* suddenly took on a completely different meaning, but rather because one specific *scientia*, namely the *philosophia naturalis* ("natural philosophy"), started playing a new role.

As the name implies, natural philosophy was the branch of academic research concerned with studying nature and reflecting on the physical world. In the natural philosophy of the sixteenth, seventeenth, and eighteenth centuries, empiricism and experimentation were accorded increasing importance. However, this did not mean that this empiricism and experimental approach were, from the outset, completely disconnected from religious beliefs. On the contrary, the intellectuals of that period attached great importance to this natural philosophy *precisely because* it seemed to offer rational support for their faith. By demonstrating the ingenuity of the laws of nature, they hoped to prove that creation could not have come into existence on its own and that God therefore had to have been involved—just like the mechanics of a watch could only be put together by a watchmaker.

In his book *The Territories of Science and Religion*, which provides a detailed account of the origin and evolution of the concept of "science," Professor Peter Harrison describes how we can find this idea even in the writings of someone like Newton:

Isaac Newton spoke for a number of his scientific contemporaries when he declared, in the celebrated General

Scholium appended to the 1715 edition of *the Principia*, that "this most elegant system of the sun, planets, and comets could not have arisen without the design and dominion of an intelligent and powerful being." Indeed for Newton, natural philosophy could not be wholly distinct from theology, for he went on to say that discourse about God "is certainly part of natural philosophy."[89]

Natural philosophy was thus the intellectual forerunner of scientific disciplines such as biology, physics, and chemistry, but initially it did not cause any kind of radical break with the prevailing religious ideas. Furthermore, the fact that science eventually grew into a separate domain of society was not because people suddenly allowed more room for purely rational ideas, but because novel religious ideas emerged. For example, the polemics between Protestants and Catholics were critical to the formation of modern science. Protestant intellectuals from the sixteenth and seventeenth centuries tried to portray the Catholic Church as a backward institution. They claimed that before the Reformation there had not been any major scientific achievements, and that they therefore were choosing to adhere to a more rational, intellectual, and pure form of Christianity. In the eighteenth century, this Protestant view was reinforced by Enlightenment philosophers such as Voltaire and d'Alembert, who criticized the connection between Catholic clergy and the monarchy. They described the Catholic Church as an institution which had deliberately hindered scientific progress. Subsequently, this premise was given a tremendous boost by nineteenth-century authors such as John William Draper, an American chemist and amateur historian, and Andrew Dickson White, an American diplomat and historian. The former published the influential *History of the Conflict between Religion and Science* in 1875, and the latter published the two-volume *History of the Warfare of Science with Theology in Christendom* in 1896. Although both books were full of inaccuracies, they contributed greatly to making this "conflict thesis" a widely held conviction. Many of the common misconceptions about the supposed anti-scientific nature of the Catholic Church— such as the image of Galileo being a misunderstood scientist persecuted by the Church from the outset—can be traced back to these works.

Thus, even though natural philosophy was originally embedded firmly within religious beliefs, it also contained some elements which gradually disconnected it from theological notions. As ever stronger emphasis was placed on rational experiment, and figures who wished to distance themselves from ecclesiastical doctrines became more strongly attracted to the field of natural philosophy, it was able to develop into a completely separate academic domain that would eventually question religion as such. In so doing, the Protestant view of "the dark ages under Catholicism" was gradually projected onto religion in general. This gave an impetus for further philosophical development of materialism and positivism. Protagonists of those philosophies argued that everything could be explained by purely physical and chemical processes and were convinced that all previous religious beliefs could be safely discarded.

Finally, around the second half of the nineteenth century, the contemporary view of science as a dimension of society that is invariably in conflict with religion emerged. During the twentieth century, the idea would live on as an apparent truism. History was viewed as an ever-upwards trend. At first, religions blinded people and made efforts to silence attempts at scientific research, but ultimately they would have to give way to science ever since the heroic efforts of enlightenment thinkers. This dichotomy, which is still deeply ingrained in our modernist thinking, is of course also the foundation of the debate about the theory of evolution.

On the different religious responses
to the theory of evolution

Opposition to Darwin's ideas is invariably regarded as the most archetypal evidence of the conflict thesis. Supposedly, religious believers find it difficult to accept that man was not created by God but evolved from earlier animal species because they subscribe to the creation stories in their sacred scriptures such as the Bible. Yet, as explained in the first chapter, it was never an ecclesiastical obligation to take the Biblical stories literally. In all religious traditions it was quite normal to interpret holy books and ancient stories symbolically, metaphorically, and allegorically.

Christian groups that strenuously cling to a literal interpretation of Bible texts are therefore a modern phenomenon. It is also no coincidence that they arose in the nineteenth century, the period in which the concept of "science" finally took its current form. Some Christians felt that their religious worldviews were being challenged. They wanted to protect them at all costs against the positivism and materialism that was becoming dominant among intellectuals, and which seemed to deny the existence of God. As a result, specific religious groups explicitly distanced themselves from certain scientific findings and demanded more room for religious perspectives.

Interestingly enough, among the most adamant Christian groups, this protective reflex often manifested in a sort of "materialist" approach to religion. Their search for truth became a mere search for *facts* instead of *wisdom*. Texts that were previously read allegorically were all of the sudden taken literally. The age-old symbolic view of the world was abandoned and the Bible came to be seen as a source of indisputable "proof."

However, we must always keep in mind that such groups certainly did not represent all Christian perceptions of evolution.[90] Even in Darwin's time, the theory was supported by some influential Christian authorities. Just a few examples include the Anglican clergyman, historian and novelist Charles Kingsley, Protestant Harvard professor Asa Gray, and the Catholic Cardinal John Henry Newman, who was canonized as a saint in 2019. In some of their texts they explicitly stated why they believed Darwin's theory did not pose any danger to their faith.

Also, those who strongly opposed Darwin's ideas certainly did not do so solely on the basis of the simple reasoning "it opposes my religious beliefs." Rather, as Professor Jon H. Roberts writes in an essay charting the differing responses to Darwin:

> Most religious thinkers who evaluated Darwin's work in the period between 1859 and about 1875 concluded that the most effective strategy they could employ in destroying the credibility of that hypothesis was to impeach its scientific credentials. A careful examination of the data of natural history, they believed, would disclose the weaknesses of evolutionary theory and thus render a sustained examination of its theological implications unnecessary. [For example, some of them referred to] the fact that previous expositions of the transmutation hypothesis had been widely condemned by natural historians. Whether espoused by reputable scientists such as Jean-Baptiste Lamarck (1744-1829) or by writers aiming at a more popular audience such as Robert Chambers (1802-71), the author of *Vestiges of the Natural History of Creation* (1844), the development hypothesis had received rough treatment at the hands of the scientific community. That prompted many religious thinkers to dismiss Darwin's work as an "old exploded theory" and to predict that his ideas would soon be consigned to the "museum of curious and fanciful speculations."[91]

Moreover, times have changed. Darwin's theories have become commonplace. We can certainly still find Christian groups who staunchly oppose the theory of evolution and support various forms of creationism (especially among certain American Evangelical communities and Jehovah's Witnesses), but it would be absurd to portray them as the norm. Even in the United States, where creationism is more prevalent than in many other countries with a large Christian population, they turn out to be a minority among Protestants and Catholics according to a 2018 survey. About a quarter of Christian Americans did indeed believe that humanity was not the result of evolutionary processes. However, this was strongly contrasted by a fifth who believed the opposite (i.e., that humanity arose solely from natural processes without any divine intervention) and *more than half* had no problem at all reconciling their belief in God with the theory of evolution (for example, by dealing metaphorically with Biblical stories as has traditionally been done, or by considering the biological laws of nature to be an inherent part of God's creation).[92]

A religious bastion such as the Catholic Church also falls into the latter group for the last several decades since the current official teachings accept the evidence for the theory as a non-contentious issue. They just do not purport a purely materialist interpretation of the theory, as if it were a denial of God's influence in creation.

The same variation can be found among Jews, for whom the Biblical creation story is obviously also an important part of their tradition. In Darwin's day, there were both Jews who opposed the theory and Jews who expressed their support, including some prominent figures. For example, Naphtali Levy, a scholar of the Torah and the Talmud, personally corresponded with Darwin. In his letters, Levy explained why he believed Jewish thought and the new evolutionary theory were compatible. Interestingly, the theory was often also popular in circles that relied heavily on Kabbalistic mysticism. A figure like the influential Rabbi Abraham Isaac Kook, who became Israel's first Ashkenazi chief rabbi, saw no problem in associating the new evolutionary perspective with Kabbalistic ideas about the spiritual development of individuals and humanity as a whole.[93]

In the last of the three great Abrahamic traditions — Islam — opinions were divided too. Some Muslims passionately proclaimed creationist views, but as early as 1888, some two years after Darwin's death, the Syrian physician and Islamic scholar Husayn al-Jisr wrote a book in which he defended the claim that Darwin's ideas did not conflict with Islamic faith or the Qur'an. According to al-Jisr, it was possible to interpret certain verses allegorically and to integrate the theory of evolution into the broader Islamic view of creation. His book was eventually endorsed by the scholars of Al-Azhar University, the foremost Islamic academic institution of the time, and was even awarded a prize by the Ottoman sultan Abdul Hamid II. In Istanbul alone the book was printed 20,000 times.[94]

Today as well, creationism is by no means the normative view among many eminent Islamic theologians. When we do encounter strong opposition to the theory of evolution in Islamic contexts, it needs to be understood as part of a wider social and political opposition to philosophical materialism and modernist ways of thinking, resembling similar tendencies in Christianity (albeit more strongly linked with resistance to Western colonialism in the case of Islam). In fact, many more parallels can be drawn between Islam and Christianity concerning the relationship between religion and science. It might be worthwhile to have a quick look at some of those parallels.

A few brief reflections on the relationship between religion and science in the Islamic world

For centuries, there was no tension whatsoever between religion and science in the Islamic world. Muslims always attached great importance to physical research and many Islamic scholars also tried to get a better understanding of God's essence by examining his creation. As a result, all kinds of rationalist disciplines were a standard part of the educational curricula in medieval Islamic universities, just like in Christian Europe. Students immersed themselves not only in subjects such as theology and law, but also in subjects such as logic, astronomy, and algebra. In fact, the latter discipline derives its name from the Arabic *al-jabr* since it was first developed by Islamic scholars.

As was the case in medieval Christianity, Muslim intellectuals considered the various fields of study and knowledge to be linked by a broad search for personal spiritual wisdom and moral balance in society. As a result, we can also point to important scientists in the history of Islam for whom critical research and rational analysis went hand in hand with their religious convictions.

A first example is the well-known, eleventh-century Ibn Sina (Avicenna). He wrote an encyclopedic work on medical sciences that, for centuries, was named *The Canon* since it was the most basic reference for any student who wanted to expand his knowledge of the field—at European, Christian universities as well, incidentally. However, like many other scholars of his day, Ibn Sina also wrote important theological treatises and Qur'anic commentaries.

Two other examples are the thirteenth-century Nasir al-Din al-Tusi and the fourteenth-century Ibn al-Shatir. More than a century and a half after they put their astronomical theories down on paper, Copernicus most probably got a hold of their work, enabling him to take important mathematical steps in his theorizing. As a result, he could move the European astronomy of his days in a different direction. Yet, in addition to being astronomers, both al-Tusi and al-Shatir were also eminent religious authorities.

In his book on Islamic science and its influence on the Renaissance, Professor George Saliba makes it clear that these two examples were not exceptional:

> [Many esteemed scientists] also held official religious positions such as judges, time keepers, and free jurists who delivered their own juridical opinions. Some of them wrote extensively on religious subjects as well, and were more famous for their religious writings than their scientific ones.[95]

The idea that religion and science inevitably conflict is therefore difficult to sustain. We have no historical, sociological, or theological basis for such a claim. This certainly does not only apply to Christianity, Judaism, and Islam. It makes little sense to engage with any tradition from this dualistic perspective.

Since both "religion" and "science" are concepts that specifically originated in a European context, it should not come as a surprise that we do not find a mention of their supposed conflict in other cultures and religions before the colonization period. As a result, academic research into the relationship between the two concepts generally focuses on historical developments in the Western and Christian world. However, those who turn to the research that nevertheless tries to look at this binary from a global perspective, will be confronted again and again with evidence of the fact that such a dualistic framework does not apply to other cultures and contexts either.[96]

A different look at the relationship between religion and science

The message of this chapter should, once again, not be misconstrued. I am certainly not trying to make the point that there has never been a conflict between "religious belief" and "rational science." Of course such conflicts have existed, but the idea that the conflict thesis was valid always and everywhere would simply be denounced by any serious historian who specializes in the history of science. In *The Cambridge Companion to Science and Religion,* Peter Harrison sums it up like this:

> When examined closely (...) the historical record simply does not bear out this model of enduring warfare. For a start, study of the historical relations between science and religion does not reveal any simple pattern at all. In so far as there is any general trend, it is that for much of the time religion has facilitated scientific endeavour and has done so in various ways. Thus, religious ideas inform and underpin scientific investigation, those pursuing science were often motivated by religious impulses, religious institutions frequently turn out to have been the chief sources of support for the scientific enterprise and, in its infancy, science established itself by appealing to religious values. This is not to say that there are no instances of conflict, but rather that these instances need to be understood within a broader context.[97]

On top of this, even if we explicitly focus on the conflicts between specific scientific findings and religious beliefs which have cropped up here and there, we must also keep in mind that science frequently conflicts with science. Both heliocentrism and Darwin's theory of evolution can serve as examples once again. Earlier in this chapter I indicated how these hypotheses were initially fought with mostly scientific—not theological— arguments. This was not because there were too many "bad" and not enough "good" scientists at the time, but simply because there is always conflict and disagreement within every discipline of knowledge. It is only when different sorts of evidence gradually accumulate that new hypotheses start convincing enough people to be taken seriously.

Some other considerations are important as well. For starters, science is not something that gradually refines our knowledge in all peace and quiet. Academics never conduct their research in a vacuum. Both they, and the policies of their research centers, are always embedded within a social and political context. Science is therefore always practiced within an ideological framework and, as a result, it is ultimately impossible to have a completely "neutral" science.

Consider, for example, the aforementioned percentages of American Christians who claim to reject the theory of evolution. When I mentioned some statistics earlier in this chapter, I based those on a 2018 survey by the Pew Research Center, but that research shows significantly different amounts than previous surveys. The reason was this: the researchers had realized that the way they phrased the question greatly influenced the answers of the survey participants. In previous years, two questions were asked. A first question tried to determine whether respondents believed humans and other life forms had always existed in their present form or whether they had instead evolved over time. If they chose the latter, they were presented with a follow-up question to assess whether they thought that evolution was merely a matter of natural processes or whether it was guided, or allowed, by God. In 2018, the researchers tried a different approach. They asked only one question with three options: do you think humans have always existed in their present form; *or* did they evolve and did God play a role in this process; *or* did they evolve without God playing any role in this process. Depending on the precise group, this sometimes resulted in a 15 to 30 percent difference. For example, the percentage of black Americans who denied evolution dropped from 59 to 27 percent, simply by rephrasing the questions.[98]

In other words, if we start from the presupposition that science and religion conflict with each other and accordingly present people a binary choice, then a seemingly objective questionnaire leads to a self-fulfilling prophecy. The results will indeed indicate that such a conflict exists, since the only possible options are mutually exclusive. However, once we add the possibility of a harmonious relationship between religion and science, it turns out to be the preference of the majority. The worldview behind an apparently "neutral" question thus determines the "facts."

This certainly does not only apply to the humanities. It is also of importance in the "hard" sciences. A good example thereof is the big bang theory. This theory was first conceived in the 1920s by the Belgian Catholic priest Georges Lemaître. Initially, his hypothesis was rejected because the idea that the universe came into being with a big bang seemed to imply that the universe could indeed be created by some divine force. Nevertheless, the whole idea was eventually accepted in the 1960s when researchers observed the cosmic microwave background, a form of electromagnetic radiation, which the theory predicted to exist because of the huge energy burst. Thus, for nearly half a century, the widespread atheistic materialism among twentieth-century academics made it difficult to accept a new, correct theory, until an accumulation of evidence forced them to.

One could of course reply that scientists are human beings after all, and therefore, indeed, never completely neutral. *However*, one might emphatically add, this does not apply to the scientific method itself. It is therefore important to follow the scientific method as precisely as possible because, when scientists succeed in doing so, their personal worldview ceases to be of importance.

Yet, the neutrality of the scientific method does not guarantee the neutrality of "science" as an aggregate of knowledge-development in society. The exact direction of scientific research is strongly determined by various factors, such as what academics believe is worth researching or not, whether they can secure funding, how much importance is attributed to potential findings, and so on. Hence, a certain ideological direction of the scientific research seems unavoidable in any context, and in this respect, it does not matter whether that context is religious, nationalist, neoliberal, socialist or atheist. Ideological convictions (religious or otherwise) will always play a role in the choice of research topics and the sociopolitical importance that people attach to the results.[99]

I of course do not wish to imply that science is inherently unreliable. There may be examples of highly problematic ideological practices within certain academic communities, but without a doubt the history of science is full of sincere efforts to gain more knowledge and truth. The fact that ideology always played and still plays an important part in what is studied, does not have to be an insurmountable problem. Despite the differences in worldview, attempts can be made to remain as objective as possible; to present facts as honestly as possible; and to make one's argumentation as solid as possible.

Everything considered, the same applies to religion. As I mentioned in the first chapter, religious truth and knowledge are not anchored in dogmas either. In religious contexts as well, we invariably find all kinds of sincere attempts to have an honest dialogue and to discover deeper truths. It is precisely for this reason that various scientific disciplines have arisen from acutely religious contexts.

Ultimately, as humans, we are all looking for "the truth" and that search is never limited to the purely rational and factual. After all, our quest is always pursued with all available means: accurate research, philosophical arguments, exchange of experiences, and deep self-reflection. Moreover, precisely because it is always a multidimensional, dynamic quest, what people perceive to be "the truth" is always subject to change within every societal context.

In this respect as well, people often pretend that science is different from religion. Science would be more adaptive to new insights, while religion stubbornly clings to one specific truth. However, the previous chapters should have made it amply clear that the truth claims of religions can differ greatly over time and throughout various cultural contexts. Just like science, religions evolve. There always are certain beliefs that disappear, while new insights emerge.

Here and there, we can certainly find certain religious groups who exacerbate the dichotomy between faith and science, and who propagate a literal reading of the mythological stories in their scriptures. Yet, even within Christianity (which is probably the only tradition in which the dichotomy has played a major role for a prolonged period), the majority of today's adherents do not experience any difficulty in aligning their faith with contemporary scientific insights.[100] They are therefore completely in line with their many ancestors, who were strongly convinced of various religious ideas, but nevertheless eagerly pursued new scientific insights.

Of course, everyone is free to opine that the scientific search in religious contexts produced a lot of nonsense while Western science, practiced on the basis of more humanistic, materialistic and positivistic views, produced great knowledge. However, what is difficult to maintain at the end of this chapter, is the idea that "faith and reason" or "religion and science" unavoidably conflict with each other because, all in all, that is a very unscientific idea.

Myth #6

Religions Are Dangerous Because Their Irrational Truth Claims Inevitably Provoke Violence

The conviction that religion is inherently inflammatory and thus should always be treated with caution surfaces in many discussions about religion. When we allow religion to set the rules of society, we hang the sword of Damocles over our heads. Sectarian violence lurks around the corner, and oppression will soon rear its head. So, the manner in which irrational religious views can incite violence obliges us to uphold a strict separation of church and state.

In the eyes of many people, therefore, the subject of violence offers one of the most important differentiations between religious and secular societies. A secular organization of society is deemed necessary for preventing religions from gaining too much influence in the public sphere, because only by ensuring religions do not impose their beliefs on others will we contain their innate proclivity toward sectarian conflict.

It certainly is also difficult to ignore the indisputable fact that religion has contributed to a great deal of bloodshed throughout history. Nevertheless, it makes sense to raise three important questions when it comes to the commonplace coupling of religion and violence.

The first question is this: how blatantly *religious* is the religious violence that people so often refer to? Religious motivations are not always easy to distinguish from political and economic interests, so how can we be certain that any instance of violence falls in one specific category?

The second question is this: does religion, *by definition*, lead people toward conflict and violence? Perhaps there are several factors that contribute to conflicts between and within various religious communities, making context of primary importance. If so, specific contexts might conversely inspire people to promote peace in their communities, thus discounting the idea that religiosity is inherently and inevitably divisive.

The third question is this: how exceptional is religion when it comes to violence? After all, if other non-religious ideologies lead to equal amounts of destruction and oppression, it seems pointless to solely focus our attention on religious beliefs.

A very good starting point to tackle these questions are the "European wars of religion" of the sixteenth and seventeenth centuries. These conflicts are invariably attributed to the intolerance displayed between Catholics and Protestants, but a renewed look at some important aspects of those conflicts can provide a very direct answer to the first question: is religious violence always so obviously religious?

Why the common description of the "European wars of religion" functions as a creation myth

When it comes to the theme of religion and violence, the wars between Catholics and Protestants present a sort of historical archetype. For many, they are self-evident examples of the inherent violence of religions, perpetuated by the defense of their irrational beliefs. In a sense they even gave rise to a "creation myth" which explains the separation of church and state. In general, the story goes something like this:

In the beginning… there was the medieval Catholic Church. This powerful religious institution forced people to believe irrational dogmas and observe stifling religious rules. After centuries of oppression, social unrest ensued. The ideas of certain freethinkers gradually took hold among larger groups of people, resulting in a widespread dissent. Within these stirrings, the "protesting" Martin Luther took the lead. He voiced explicit criticisms against the Pope and the Church. He also promoted translations of the Bible, so people could read the scriptures themselves and call their faith into question. His ideas fell on fertile ground, not only among the populace, but also with political leaders. It was not long before the Catholic Church reacted, however, resulting in conflicts between Protestants and Catholics that quickly degenerated into a fierce and violent struggle. More than a century of religious wars ensued but, luckily, the fanatical theological disputes were eventually curbed by political treaties that defined the boundaries of nation-states and subjected the influence of religion to those new state structures. Thus, a crucial step was taken toward the formation of our modern, secularized society. In short: the establishment of the European nation-states resulted in a kind of "clearing of the religious minefield."

Different variations of this story abound, making it sound very familiar to most people, but this description of religious violence versus secular peace in early modernity becomes questionable once it is subjected to critical analysis. For example, in his book *The Myth of Religious Violence*, Professor William T. Cavanaugh very thoroughly explains how the various findings of contemporary academic historical research paint a very different picture. If religious disagreements were the primary cause of the conflict, Cavanaugh rightly argues, this would logically lead to three consequences:

1. Members of the same religious community fought only (or at least mainly) against groups of other religious communities.
2. Those who held one religious belief did not fight side by side with those who held a different belief.
3. If the religious differences were large enough within certain segments of a specific community, new factions arose and clashed.

The problem is that none of these consequences are witnessed in the historical facts. Let us begin with a couple of examples of hostility within the same religious communities. The latter half of the Thirty Years' War was essentially a struggle between the Habsburgs and the House of Bourbon, the two great Catholic dynasties of Europe; in the English Civil War, the main opponents—the Puritans and the Laudians—were two factions of the Anglican Church. Another extremely interesting case is the fact that in 1525, Catholic France regularly formed alliances with the Islamic Turks against the emperor of the Holy Roman Empire, Charles V.

That last example also demonstrates that religious opponents did indeed fight side by side. To give a few more illustrations: Cardinal Richelieu and Catholic France intervened in the Thirty Years' War on the side of Lutheran Sweden; the majority of Emperor Charles' soldiers were mercenaries and included a large number of Protestants; and Protestant and Catholic peasants united in dozens of revolts, at times mobilizing about 40,000 people. The most famous of these revolts were the Croquant rebellions, which are doubly interesting because the policies of this association explicitly stated that its members should set aside their ecclesiastical differences.

Lastly, religious factions also sometimes did not fight each other at all when we would expect them to do so, if the assumption were correct that religion was the sole driving force behind conflicts. For example, although there were plenty of doctrinal disputes between Calvinists and Lutherans, in the end, no Lutheran prince ever went to war against a Calvinist prince.

These are just a handful of examples from a very extensive list enumerated by Professor Cavanaugh. It is therefore not a question of a few minor exceptions, but of profound paradoxes that, taken together, raise a difficult question: if "religion" does not adequately explain the events we consistently refer to as "wars of religion," how else should we explain those conflicts?

This too is clarified by historical research. The rise of modern, secular nation-states was not really the solution, but rather the *cause* of the wars. Even before the Reformation, a complex social and political dynamic had reared its head, making old centers of power collapse and new centers of power emerge. Conflicts erupted between the various factions of feudal elites, city dignitaries and ecclesiastical leaders, all striving for a new or reinforced status and position.

This also sheds new light on the ensuing political efforts to calm the violence.

> The Peace of Augsburg—which gave each prince the power to determine the ecclesial affiliation of his subjects—was not the state's solution to religious violence, but rather represented the victory of one set of state-building elites over another. As Richard Dunn remarks about the Peace of Augsburg: "The German princes, Catholic and Lutheran, had in effect ganged up against the Habsburgs. They had observed, correctly enough, that Charles V had been trying not only to crush Protestantism but to increase Habsburg power and check the centrifugal tendencies within the empire. The princes, both Lutheran and Catholic, had also been trying to turn the Reformation crisis to their personal advantage, by asserting new authority over their local churches, tightening ecclesiastical patronage, and squeezing more profit from church revenues." (…) Much of the violence of the so-called wars of religion is explained in terms of the resistance of local elites to the state-building efforts of monarchs and emperors.[101]

It is important to realize that Cavanaugh's presentation of the historic evidence is not an attempt to advance the equally untenable proposition that the European wars of the sixteenth and seventeenth centuries had no religious motive whatsoever and were merely a matter of politics. Nor does he lay all the blame on the new state structures in the hopes of sparing the church. In fact, his portrayal is quite candid regarding the involvement of various religious ideas and institutions surrounding the violence. As such, he merely wants to demonstrate the inherent complexity and entanglement of a multitude of factors, since the historical facts clearly show that various forms of power struggle led to a recalibration of the existing structures, with the gradual absorption of the church *into* the state acting as a driving force behind this process.

Accordingly, Cavanaugh concludes that the well-known story "is at best a distorted and one-dimensional narrative; at worst, it eliminates so many of the relevant political, economic, and social factors as to be rendered false."[102]

This is not merely a minor correction in the commonplace portrayal of these historical conflicts. It offers a severe blow to basic assumptions underlying the dominant worldview, and, as a result, it challenges the power structures which are legitimized on the basis of that assumption since it reveals that the modern nation-state offers no guarantee against fanatical aggression. These historic conflicts only managed to shift the center of power. They transferred the capacity to determine which violence is legitimate and which is not to another group of people. Thus, the rise of the modern state did not create a more peaceful Europe, but it did alter what people were willing to fight and die for. To modern sensibilities, killing in the name of God became something incomprehensible, while killing in the name of a homeland, nation, state, or democracy became something laudable.

In short, the new status quo after the European wars of the sixteenth and seventeenth centuries was not the containment of religion but, as historian John Bossy called it, "a migration of the holy."[103] During the first half of the twentieth century, nationalism—and the accompanying worship of "the people" and "the nation"—became the driving force behind two world wars, which together claimed the lives of some 100 million people, making them by far the most costly conflicts in history.

So, even in one of the most typical historical examples, "religious violence" cannot be reduced to its religious elements. For any serious historian, it is of course self-evident that we should always consider all the various political, social, cultural, military, and economic factors when discussing complex conflicts. The importance of religion should certainly not be underestimated, but simply establishing a direct cause-effect relationship between religion and violence is nonsensical. Whether we discuss the Crusades, the occupation of Palestine, or the violence in Kashmir, the religious elements are always inseparable from the political, economic, and territorial elements.

The simple and rather obvious idea—that one must take all factors into account to get a sufficiently clear view of any conflict—leads us to the second question that was raised at the beginning of this chapter: does religion *inevitably* lead to violence? If the violence is contextually determined, perhaps there are also specific factors and circumstances that sometimes lead religious people and communities down a different path, toward peace.

To delve deeper into this matter, I turn to a second archetypal example of "religious violence," albeit from a very different time and region: the massacres which accompanied the split between India and Pakistan.

On the fact that religion regularly leads to peace

When the British colonizers relinquished power to the people of British India in August 1947, this was accompanied by the partition of the region into Pakistan and India. As a result, many Indian Muslims moved to Pakistan and, conversely, many Pakistani Hindus moved to India. This eventually became a mass migration involving about fifteen million people. Horrific scenes played out on both sides of the border. About one million people died.[104]

However, theological issues played no role. This makes sense, considering the root cause of the related violence had nothing to do with different conceptualizations of God or a call to holy war. The conflict was firmly embedded within the nationalist politics of the time. Once it became clear that they would succeed in shaking off the yoke of the long, brutal colonization by the British, people began to doubt the future political formation of India. Many Muslims feared that they would be discriminated against, since they would be a minority in a country that was predominantly Hindu. The political friction eventually segregated the country: the Muslim-majority areas became Pakistan, the Hindu-majority areas became India.

This political fracture and the ensuing communal violence greatly distressed Mohandas Karamchand Gandhi, who, in previous years, had become the leader of the most massive decolonization movement the country had ever witnessed. For years he had worked to overcome the military logic of the British occupiers with campaigns that focused on sociopolitical peace, as well as personal, inner peace. To this day, the Mahatma remains world famous for his method of active nonviolence, which was explicitly grounded in Hindu frameworks. Even more so, as politically active as he was, he often primarily emphasized his religious outlook. In the introduction to his autobiography, *The Story of My Experiments with Truth*, he stated this without reserve:

What I want to achieve—what I have been striving and pining to achieve these thirty years—is self-realization, to see God face to face, to attain Moksha. I live and move

135

and have my being in pursuit of this goal. All that I do by way of speaking and writing, and all my ventures in the political field, are directed to this same end. But as I have all along believed that what is possible for one is possible for all, my experiments have not been conducted in the closet, but in the open; and I do not think that this fact detracts from their spiritual value. There are some things which are known only to oneself and one's Maker. These are clearly incommunicable. The experiments I am about to relate are not such. But they are spiritual, or rather moral; for the essence of religion is morality.[105]

The strongest expressions of Gandhi's acute religiosity were his fasts in Calcutta and Delhi. During the massive population movements of 1947, these metropolises were plagued by severe violence. Gandhi publicly announced that he would fast to death unless the various factions ceased their atrocities. In both cities the fighting stopped after three days. As far as Gandhi was concerned, this was not merely a matter of political tactics. He portrayed his fasting as a predominantly spiritual act. During his last fast in Delhi he addressed the people accordingly:

> With God as my supreme, and sole counsellor, I felt that I must take the decision without any other adviser. [...] Hence, I urge everybody dispassionately to examine the purpose and let me die, if I must, in peace which I hope is ensured. Death for me would be a glorious deliverance rather than that I should be a helpless witness of the destruction of India, Hinduism, Sikhism and Islam. [...] I am in God's hands. [...] This is essentially a testing time for all of us. [...] The fast is a process of self-purification.[106]

Despite the calm that his fasts brought to the cities and the surrounding areas, simmering tensions persisted and the violence, still raging in other regions, would only completely disappear when Gandhi was murdered on January 30, 1948—not by a fanatical Muslim who wanted to kill Gandhi because he was a Hindu, but by a Hindu who felt that Gandhi demanded too many political concessions from Hindus. His death sent a shock wave through the country and ushered in a fifteen-year period of communal peace.

However, an understandable focus on Gandhi's role during this tumultuous period often causes people to lose sight of other important peacemakers. Gandhi most certainly did not stand alone in his endeavors. Throughout the vast territory over which the British ruled (that is, present-day Afghanistan, Pakistan, Kashmir, India, and Bangladesh), other charismatic figures from different religious backgrounds gathered large crowds in peaceful protests.

One of the more significant of these was Abdul Ghaffar Khan. This imposing man has been called the "Frontier Gandhi" because he tried to spread the message of nonviolence in the western borderlands of British India—a region that now partly belongs to Pakistan as well as Afghanistan. Since Abdul Ghaffar Khan was a Muslim, his own form of active nonviolence drew inspiration largely from the Qur'an and the life stories of the Prophet Muhammad. While he spent much longer periods in captivity than Gandhi (and often in much harsher conditions), he still managed to build history's first nonviolent "army." With his movement of the *Khudai Khidmatgar* ("servants of God") he mobilized 100,000 nonviolent "soldiers." They engaged in various forms of peaceful activism and civil disobedience to denounce injustice and drive out the colonizing forces.

Such figures and their specific approach to sociopolitical reform, at once practical and spiritual, were a profound inspiration to people like Martin Luther King, who once wrote:

Gandhi was probably the first person in history to lift the love ethic of Jesus above mere interaction between individuals to a powerful and effective social force on a large scale. (...) It was in this Gandhian emphasis on love and nonviolence that I discovered the method for social reform that I had been seeking. (...) The intellectual and moral satisfaction that I failed to gain from the utilitarianism of Bentham and Mill, the revolutionary methods of Marx and Lenin, the social contract theory of Hobbes, the "back to nature" optimism of Rousseau, and the superman philosophy of Nietzsche, I found in the nonviolent resistance philosophy of Gandhi. I came to feel that this was the only morally and practically sound method open to oppressed people in their struggle for freedom.[107]

King did not blanketly copy Gandhi's active nonviolence. He produced his own approach based on his Christian tradition and the teachings of the Bible. That is why his famous *I have a dream* speech contains several references to verses from the Old as well as the New Testament, and why he ends the speech with the words of a religious anthem, which was often sung by black Americans:

When we allow freedom to ring—when we let it ring from every city and every hamlet, from every state and every city, we will be able to speed up that day when all of God's children, black men and white men, Jews and Gentiles, Protestants and Catholics, will be able to join hands and sing in the words of the old Negro spiritual: "Free at last, Free at last, Great God a-mighty, we are free at last."[108]

When we talk about figures like Mahatma Gandhi, Abdul Ghaffar Khan and Martin Luther King, we are not talking about people who are relegated to the sidelines of history. They are, without a doubt, three protagonists of active nonviolence in the twentieth century. They were instrumental in breaking the stranglehold of grotesque injustices their communities were subjected to by modern, secular governments. Each of them also had an obvious religious drive, strongly rooted in their respective Hindu, Islamic and Christian traditions. They can therefore be regarded as textbook cases of the fact that religion can kindle people's capacity to stand up against the prevailing militaristic atmosphere and can stimulate people to strive for the possibility of peaceful conflict resolution.

Once again, this does not only apply to modern religious figures and groups. It would make little sense to think that we will only encounter such peaceful attitudes among people who, based on contemporary assumptions, have left behind the old, traditional violence of religion. Many historical examples could be given to this end as well. Just one would be the encounter of Saint Francis and the Egyptian sultan Al-Kamil, a nephew of the famous Saladin.

This incident is usually quoted to illustrate the peacefulness of the thirteenth-century Christian mystic. After all, Saint Francis' strong insistence on peace and openness is one of the reasons behind him being one of the most important reformers in Christian history, and additionally why he currently functions as a kind of Christian patron saint of interfaith dialogue.

It certainly is a captivating story. During one of the many crusades, Francis served as a counterexample to the displays of military prowess in his day and age. Barefoot and dressed in nothing but a coarse tunic, he managed to traverse a turbulent war zone unscathed, and was granted an audience with the sultan.

Sadly, we have no idea how the meeting proceeded. The descriptions of this meeting in the original sources are wrapped in too many layers of hagiography. There is, however, no doubt that the encounter did in fact take place, as it was described in several independent sources hailing from both Franciscans and the Crusaders, each with their own interpretations of the event. Also, although it is unclear what they exactly discussed, it is known that Francis was favorably received by the sultan. Moreover, the sultan ensured safe passage for Francis to visit the tomb of Christ. Francis would eventually spend many months in Islamic territory and, ever since, the Franciscan order was officially allowed to be present in the Holy Land by the Islamic authorities. Francis' nonviolent approach thus took him and his monastic brothers much further than the warmongering took the Crusaders.

We will probably never be completely certain of Francis' motivation owing to the limited historical material, but in any case, he met the sultan and neither of them felt it necessary to cut the other's throat. However, when this historical event is recounted today, people often forget to mention that Francis was not the only man of peace in the room. Usually, it is simply assumed that the Muslims were just as aggressive as the Crusaders, but this was not the case. Sultan Al-Kamil was known for his great tolerance—even among the Christians who were living in the region at the time. He made several peace proposals, even after winning battles, but those proposals were repeatedly pushed aside by the Christian militia leaders, even though they included a provision that Christian pilgrims would be assured safe passage to Jerusalem. The sultan's proposal would have offered a solution for the initial (theoretical) reason behind the crusade, yet the crusaders remained insistent on warfare.[109]

A hypothesis: Saint Francis as a medieval peace activist
In the many descriptions of Saint Francis' encounter with the sultan, an interesting possibility is often overlooked: perhaps we can see Francis as a kind of anti-militarist activist. In fact, quite a few arguments support this hypothesis. For example, we know that, in his younger years, he dreamed of becoming a heroic knight but that two profound experiences eventually convinced him to reconsider: being imprisoned after joining a fight between

the cities of Assisi and Perugia, and a spiritual vision that he experienced when he hoped to join the army of Walter III of Brienne. As such, his initial decision to leave the world behind and to become a mendicant monk was not merely a choice to live a life of poverty based on his insight into the transience of wealth. It is also closely linked with an epiphany concerning the madness of violence, strife, and war.

Moreover, it seems quite unlikely that Francis' pacifism, which made him decide to seek out the sultan and engage in dialogue, which starkly contrasted the violence of the Crusaders, was an entirely isolated phenomenon. Such figures are often portrayed as unique people who did something completely exceptional in a way that seems almost incomprehensible. When we consider the realities of life, however, that seems highly improbable. Ideas never exist in a vacuum. Therefore, it would be rather strange if Francis' intention came out of the blue. It makes more sense that a spirit of pacifism and anti-militarism was alive and well in those days, and that Francis partly embodied this spirit.

So, while the history of religion is full of stories of belligerent rulers, we can find just as many stories about peace seekers who invoked religious principles to transcend the conventional rhetoric of war. In addition, I have limited myself to some considerations that explicitly address the themes of violence and peace. Hence, this chapter does not focus on the countless forms of care for the poor and the sick that are connected to religious motivations, even though these would also be good examples of the manner in which religion orients an enormous number of people toward mercy, reconciliation, and healing.

This does not mean that religion only produces positive effects or that we can claim it is never the foundation upon which malicious acts have been committed. That would be absurd. Of course, we can point to many disastrous elements of oppression, exclusion, and violence throughout the history of all larger religious traditions. The point this chapter hopes to elucidate is simply that religion, like any other dimension of society, has the capacity to lead us in multiple directions. Just as politics can lead to emancipation or oppression, religion can lead to peace or war. Just as an economic policy can lead to redistribution or exploitation, a religious approach can lead to inclusion or exclusion. Just as cultural customs can lead to acceptance or marginalization of minorities, religious practices can lead to freedom or coercion. Just as in politics, economics, and culture, everything depends on the interaction between a multitude of interpretations and on how various power dynamics play out. The same is true when it comes to religion.

For some, however, this cannot suffice as a final argument. One specific characteristic of religion would make it different from various other political ideologies: *absolutism*. Since religion claims a transcendent, divine truth, it would have a unique and inherent tendency to forcibly impose its own views, and thus, by necessity, silence the views of others.

Considering the analysis that was already presented in the first chapter, this idea is rather difficult to substantiate. "Divine truths" or "a belief in something transcendent" are not at the center of every religious context, therefore they are not the determining factor of religiosity. However, I do not want to simply discount the argument. The suggestion that religious ideas are inherently more dangerous than non-religious ideas because of their propensity for absolutism deserves a more profound response. Moreover, it leads us directly to the third question raised at the beginning of this chapter: are religions truly unique in this regard?

On secular absolutism

Most certainly, people have sometimes been persecuted, humiliated, and murdered in the name of some god. Yet, all kinds of grotesque injustice and aggression are legitimized in the name of entirely secular ideas just as well. In this respect, one can obviously make references to devastating ideologies such as Nazism, fascism, or Stalinist communism. The fact that they are jointly responsible for tens of millions of deaths needs little explanation. In the first case, there was the absolutism of a secular devotion to the Führer and the German people. In the second case, there was the absolutism of a male leadership ideal that wiped out anything standing in its way, religious or not. In the latter case, there was the explicitly atheistic absolutism of a centralist state structure which attempted to eliminate every possible form of dissent. Moreover, we can easily supplement these well-known examples with those from other ideologies, which are perhaps less often mentioned, but whose destruction was certainly no less real, such as the neoliberalism of Pinochet, the nationalism of Milošević, or the capitalism of colonization.

Even concepts such as "human rights" and "democracy" can lead to forms of absolutism that cause a significant amount of oppression and violence. This might seem less obvious at first, but all kinds of examples can be offered from well-known conflicts. Less than ten years after the Universal Declaration of Human Rights, a disastrous war broke out in Vietnam. Chemical weapons like napalm destroyed 3.8 million hectares of farmland, killed 13,000 animals, and killed more than a thousand farmers.[110] This war, which lasted for two decades and killed approximately two million people, was presented as a war aimed at preserving world peace, because according to the United States government, democracy had to be protected by stopping the communist threat.[111] Twenty years later, the United States backed El Salvador's brutal and murderous military dictatorship, not only with words, but also with very tangible actions, such as financial support and—out of the public eye— the training of paramilitary groups which committed a huge amount of atrocities. This was regularly described as providing assistance to "a fledgling democracy."[112] In the decades that followed, this superpower—which invariably claims to be a stalwart of human rights—would continue to support various dictatorships. An absurd example of this was seen in 2013, when general Abdel Fattah el-Sisi came to power in Egypt after a successful military coup which ousted the democratically elected President Mohamed Morsi. El-Sisi immediately committed gross human rights violations, such as killing at least 900 Morsi supporters, and silencing any form of protest.[113] However, John Kerry, the US Secretary of State at the time, supported el-Sisi's coup by describing it as "a restoration of democracy."[114]

Some may argue that democratic values and a focus on human rights play no role in such events and dynamics because, time and again, these values are overshadowed by sinister economic motives and a lust for power. The idea would thus be that important ethical principles are abused, sometimes even consciously, to eventually serve the interests of the powerful, contrary to the wishes of the public. However, if that is indeed the case in such examples of violence, why should not the same be true for conflicts involving religious extremists? Why not just as easily claim that religion is often abused toward political ends?

It is difficult to consistently uphold such an argument. Let us take the Islamic terrorism of the first two decades of the twenty-first century as an example. We cannot discard this phenomenon by stating that the violence of extremists has nothing to do with "real" Islam, because "real" Islam is solely focused on peace. Anyone who holds Islamic mercy in high esteem simply cannot hide behind the proposition that groups like Al-Qaeda and Daesh are "un-Islamic," because the fact of the matter remains that these extremist groups legitimize their actions using Islamic terms. Regardless of whether they do so in a consistent manner, or whether they have any authority on a theological level, they certainly describe themselves as Muslim groups. So, whether we like it or not, Al Qaeda and Daesh are also a part of the Islamic world, just as the Ku Klux Klan and the Lord's Resistance Army are part of the Christian world. As such, it does not make a lot of sense to protect religions from every possible dark side, and to pretend that they "in principle" or "at their core" do not promote such aberrations. However, when we acknowledge this about religions, we must also acknowledge the same about the moral and ethical frameworks of modernist worldviews and ideologies. It is not appropriate to exempt democracy, human rights, and humanitarian intervention from any kind of criticism when they produce violence by simply stating that "in principle" or "at their core" they have a peaceful outlook. Anyone who holds liberty, equality, and fraternity in high esteem, cannot hide behind the proposition that military invasions "only serve economic interests." Not only do politicians and media pundits rely on all kinds of norms and values to legitimize wars and invasions, those same norms and values also strongly mobilize the public. Regardless of whether this is done in a consistent manner, secular societies often present themselves as humane, freedom-loving, democratic nations — even though many policies are often quite inhumane; even though the freedom of many people is severely impeded; and even though democracy is often the last thing they truly spread around the world.

No matter how noble, all modern secular ideologies, norms, and values can become as absolutist as any religious belief. It is therefore necessary that we reconsider the relationship between religion and violence, and that we avoid the platitudes surrounding the topic. To understand the many vicious cycles of violence in the world, we will have to look beyond religion and search for deeper patterns.

A different look at the relationship
between religion and violence

Violent conflicts between different communities are often fueled by a far-reaching "us-versus-them" mentality. The group to which one belongs is seen as an honorable "we," full of truth and purity, while "they" are seen as inferior and impure. There is often an accompanying feeling that "we" are under threat and must therefore protect our integrity against the intrusion of "the enemy." As this us-versus-them thinking grows, it can eventually lead to such strong forms of dehumanization, that it becomes justified to attack, imprison, and kill all of "them."

Such a dualistic worldview, which serves to divide people into groups who are either with us or against us, is commonly associated with religious traditions—and more specifically so with the Abrahamic religions. It is also undeniable that Jews, Christians, and Muslims exhibited particularly powerful us-versus-them mentalities at various points in history. On theological and cultural grounds, "us" was often associated with holiness, and "them" with demonic evil—sometimes even calling for the complete destruction of the diabolical other.

However, as this chapter has tried to clarify, modern and secular ideologies are in no way less prone to such thinking. The us-versus-them mentality of secular contexts can sometimes even be exceptionally strong. It only uses different labels, such as the Nazi dichotomy of *Übermenschen* and *Untermenschen*; such as the division of capitalists and communists during the Cold War; such as the artificial construction of "the West" versus "Islam," which, to this day, continues to add fuel to the fire of the so-called "war on terror."

The danger of absolutism therefore is not an inherent problem of transcendent concepts, rather it is a problem inherent in claiming to *be* transcendent. Concepts like "democracy," "human rights," and "the nation" are all transcendent concepts, just like "freedom," "equality," and "fraternity." In themselves they can be truly beautiful aims. However, those who present themselves as their final master become dangerous. Whoever thinks that his rationality is *the* rationality; that his form of humanism is *the* humane approach; and that his vision of the future is *the* inevitable way forward, sees himself as God. Hence, it is not *belief* in a god which is the problem, but rather the way some people try to position themselves as one. Whether they do so in religious or secular contexts does not matter much in this respect.

Whoever claims the transcendent for himself ultimately usurps a higher position and thereby ironically rids the transcendent of its transcendence. In other words: only when people proclaim to be transcendent themselves, only when they pretend to "know" with certainty what the transcendent "wants," only then does the danger of oppressive violence arise, because, at that very moment, they place themselves above "the others" and start seeing them as inferior. Therein lies the germ of problematic us-versus-them thinking.

Of course, several other dynamics are also of great importance when we talk about violence and oppression. Many books have justly been written about those dynamics. However, what has been discussed in this chapter can suffice for the purposes of this book since we can conclude that religion does not have a monopoly on any of those dynamics; not even on those that drive the aggression and false sense of superiority of an absolutist faith.

Myth #7

A Secular Society Is Completely Different (and Inherently Better) Than a Religious Society

"The world becoming more worldly" is one of the more poetic descriptions of secularization. It succinctly reflects how religious institutions are losing their influence in society, how religion is becoming ever more a private matter, and how religious beliefs are consequently subordinated to prevailing political views.

In this and many other descriptions of secularism, it is striking that the concept is typically not sharply delineated, but rather presented as a contrast. As such, attempts at defining "the secular" mostly result in a straightforward juxtaposition: the secular is *the opposite* of the religious. A secular worldview is seen as spiritually free and scientifically sound, *in contrast to* religion. A secular society is seen as not hierarchical and not dogmatic, *in contrast to* a religious society. Secular politics are seen as rational and nonviolent *in contrast to* politics influenced by religion.

The previous chapters made it amply clear why such a starting point is problematic: the assumed negative criteria are not universal traits of religion at all. One can, of course, enumerate various examples of religious groups who are based on a dogmatic faith; who turn away from scientific findings; who are mobilized by a hierarchical leadership; and who incite violence against people of other faiths because of their intolerance. However, there is no reason to see these examples as the norm. The various manifestations of religion are too diverse to allow for a simple reduction to such phenomena. Overall, no single religion is restricted to elements of "zealous beliefs," "hierarchical coercion" or "resistance to science."

On top of this, we may wonder whether these elements apply just as often to secular ideologies, because if that turns out to be the case, it might become extremely difficult to maintain the sharp contrast between the religious and the secular. In this chapter I will therefore briefly review all the myths one last time, but now pose the question whether these characteristics can also be encountered in secular contexts as well.

Why the secular often exhibits all the characteristics normally associated with the religious

Examples of secular beliefs and rules of conduct

Secular ideologies often present themselves as purely rational and objective, but anyone who takes a deeper look will quickly be confronted with strong convictions that are rooted in a firm belief system. What is more, such belief systems are often based on transcendent concepts. For example, concepts such as "the nation" or "the people" are transcendent in many respects. They transcend the individuals who belong to them, connecting them to a "deeper reality"—that is, a reality which people believe has already existed before them and will continue to exist after them, despite no objective indication of such a reality. After all, national borders are not naturally carved out in the earth, and the divisions between communities and peoples have been subject to constant change throughout history. In addition, "the nation" and "the people" are also linked to a plethora of heroic stories that are based on few, if any, facts, but which emphasize the greatness of the respective nation and people. Does that mean that any form of nationalism is, by definition, a religious ideology?

The same goes for a concept like "human rights." It is a transcendent ethical concept since we assume that human rights are universal and are based on a self-contained, inherent human dignity that is by definition "given" to

149

everyone. In a modernist worldview, we may not name who or what "gave" us this dignity, but that does not make the idea any less transcendent. So, is the Charter of the United Nations a religious document?

Or how should we engage with a concept like "the invisible hand of the market?" We can hardly call it a purely immanent, materialistic, and humanistic idea. Some economists will argue that "the invisible hand" is only a metaphor for the various processes that spontaneously manifest themselves when people trade with one another. However, while in theory it might be metaphorical, in practice many policymakers appear to regard it as a kind of transcendent reality. They consciously try to prevent a disruption of the market because they strongly believe that its "natural functioning" produces the best society. Does this imply that many (neo)liberal politicians have a religious view of the economy?

Such transcendent principles also give rise to many precepts and rituals. Nationalism is invariably accompanied by flags and anthems intended to remind people of their mythology using powerful symbols; to celebrate our human rights, certain days of the year are given special significance, such as the International Women's Day (March 8) or the International Day of Peace (September 21); and when we observe economists from a distance while they are tracking all kinds of numbers on the Wall Street stock exchange, accompanied by their spasmodic bodily movements, we can hardly escape the feeling that we are witnessing a group of people who are trying to control the market with magical rituals.[115]

These are, of course, just a few examples. We could give many others from different dimensions of society, but these can suffice to make the point that secular environments are rife with faith and ritual behavior.

To believe in God or not

When such examples of secular faith are cited, it may be tempting for some to create a distinction between the religious and the secular on the basis of a belief in God. For example, one could acknowledge that secular ideologies are indeed often guided by a certain belief system but add that at least they are not based on a belief in some god. The important difference would then reside in the fact that a secular person can always remain critical and is not obliged to acknowledge a divine truth. However, such a statement simply catapults us back to the very first chapter of this book. So, as a quick reminder: in that initial chapter I outlined various approaches toward the divine and explained that not all religions are based on a belief in a (personal) God. Some traditions even turned out to include atheistic tendencies. I also explained that we can refer to many important religious figures who did not assume something simply because it was prescribed. People often relate to God because of personally experiencing a divine essence and not so much because they uncritically accepted the tenets of their tradition.

Examples of secular hierarchy

In contemporary secular societies, governments and corporations are undoubtedly the two most powerful types of institutions, wielding the greatest influence over everyone's life. On a daily basis, people adhere to the laws set by the government and are dependent on all kinds of products made by large corporations. Moreover, an enormous amount of the working population is employed by these institutions, and thus spend a large part or even most of their waking hours in them.

In Chapter 2, I mentioned in passing that we mainly spend our lives in hierarchical structures because, generally speaking, both nation-states and corporations are organized hierarchically to a strong degree. Even democratic nation-states still have a layered form of representative democracy, with various levels of power in the parliamentary and governmental institutions. In large companies, the hierarchical element is generally even more explicit. Usually, there is no talk of democracy at all as they are mostly managed top-down by a CEO and a board of directors.

Other possibilities are certainly conceivable. A good example would be anarchism. Of course, I am not talking about the caricature that the word "anarchism" usually evokes today: people who squat in abandoned houses, who resist any form of authority and who break the windows of shops during protests. Originally, anarchism (or more correctly: anarcho-syndicalism) was a political movement that grew out of socialist and communist ideas. It wanted to offer an alternative to the capitalist system, but, unlike most communist groups, without replacing it with a new centralist regime. Anarchism therefore tried to work bottom-up by uniting everyone in different cooperatives, which put production in the hands of the people. Such a cooperative might oversee a school, organize agriculture, offer public maintenance of the municipality and so on. In each cooperative, all members had a direct vote, and within the cooperatives representatives were elected to collaborate with the other cooperatives when necessary. The final aim was a completely decentralized political structure of society. Historically speaking, anarcho-syndicalism did not merely remain a utopian theory. These basic principles were in fact thoroughly experimented with, for example in the 1930s when a large part of Spain was run anarchically. However, this web of anarcho-syndicalist groups was violently crushed, first by the communist party and the conservative bourgeoisie, and later by the fascistic dictatorship of Franco.

Whatever we think about it in practice, at least in theory we cannot but admit that anarcho-syndicalism is by far the most egalitarian and democratic political movement. However, contemporary nation-states certainly are not organized in such a manner. In terms of the economy, we are even further removed from any type of grassroots democracy, since our globalized economy is mainly determined by centrally organized multinational corporations with multilevel power structures, which frequently exploit the people at the bottom of the pyramid.

Hence, values such as liberty, equality, and fraternity might be invoked as the basic principles of post-revolutionary secular societies, but most people's lives are indeed governed by firm hierarchies. Even more so, when we really try to apply "liberty, equality, and fraternity" in a consistent manner (for example by advocating a more anarcho-syndicalist model of society and organizing ourselves in a cooperative), we are usually viewed with disdain. If, subsequently, we continue with our plans, we might even become obstructed by the dominant political and economic groups in society.

Considering all of this, it is also striking how the equivalent of a "top layer of priests" is never far away within the accepted hierarchies of secular societies. In business environments, for example, they are abundantly present. In the average company, every now and then a consultant is recruited to provide some form of spiritual guidance (for example, by motivating teams to go back to work after major downsizing), to hear confessions (for example, through compliance assessments), to explain the moral precepts (for example, through brainstorming sessions about the mission and vision of the company) or to make predictions for the future (for example, through an info session about the most important business trends a company needs to take into account). Some highly esteemed consultants who write best-selling how-to books are even addressed with an explicitly religious term such as "management guru."

Again, we could easily offer more examples, but these illustrations sufficiently clarify that hierarchy is found just as much (and given just as much emphasis) in secular institutions as in religious communities.

Examples of unclear boundaries between the secular and the religious

Chapter 3 presented a series of examples that showed how the boundaries between different traditions are often very permeable because it is not always possible to neatly distinguish one religion from another. The same is true, however, of the boundary between the religious and the secular.

A first example is Unitarian Universalism. Worldwide, this religious group has more than a thousand congregations and more than 800,000 members. It came into being in 1961 after a merger of two Christian churches, both of which propagated strongly pluralistic ideas since the eighteenth and nineteenth centuries. By now, there is little trace left of explicit Christian beliefs, though one is certainly allowed to uphold them because the adherents see Unitarian Universalism as a religion which embraces all belief systems. As such, members of the church are free to believe—or not to believe—whatever they want. Atheists are also expressly welcomed. The rituals of Unitarian Universalist churches portray a similar openness: the congregations come together to freely discuss spiritual issues and within their gatherings there is often an eclectic mix of elements from various traditions.

So, characteristics which are often attributed to our (post) modern secular society, such as an emphasis on personal freedom and transcending religious differences, are sometimes explicitly adopted by contemporary religious movements.

For a second example, we can have a look at a group with an opposing dynamic since it explicitly emerged out of secular principles, but eventually became religious: the Religion of

Humanity. This religious group was founded by Auguste Comte, the nineteenth-century mathematician and philosopher who first articulated the tenets of modern positivism and thus became one of the foremost protagonists of the idea that only empiricism, rationality, and a strict scientific approach can lead to valid knowledge and progress. Throughout the nineteenth and twentieth centuries, all kinds of philosophical leanings were imbued with variants of this positivist worldview.

As such, Comte's influence on contemporary ideologies cannot be underestimated. His positivist church, on the other hand, was less successful. Comte was convinced that after the breakup of religion, people would still need places of worship where they could build community ties and strengthen their ethical character. Therefore, he developed a religion centered on altruism, order, progress, and the worship of humanity as "the New Supreme Great Being." This endeavor was not simply a matter of propagating a few novel secular-spiritual concepts, but was also accompanied by the development of churches, rituals, sacraments, and a group of priests. Comte even wrote a catechism, in which he laid down the principles of his religion. One of the architects of modern rationalistic thinking thus very consciously tried to develop a religion of his own, though internal tensions and schisms soon reduced this Religion of Humanity to a very small community. Nevertheless, many of its humanistic ideas influenced the nineteenth-century intelligentsia and live on in various forms of present-day humanism.

Hence, both Unitarian Universalism and Comte's Religion of Humanity demonstrate very well that the boundaries between the religious and the secular can sometimes be very fluid.

Examples of secular spirituality with religious characteristics
Chapter 4 explained how contemporary postural yoga can be understood as a form of religious syncretism. Through various

cultural dynamics, a concept which originated within the Hindu tradition found its way into the mainstream spirituality of personal growth. The search for the unity of one's inner self with a divine primal source has been transformed into a practice to restore the balance between mind and body. Even though yoga as a concept has deeply religious roots, its reinterpretation through the lens of physical culture eventually made it an established ritual part of various contemporary spiritual circles in Western countries.

The same kind of syncretism can also be observed in the way the image of the Buddha is used in Western countries today. In cities like Paris, London, or New York we can hardly walk into a spa without being greeted by all kinds of gently smiling Buddhas. The Buddha thus became the prophet of inner balance (or, perhaps even one step further, the global god of wellness). That is also why flowers are placed in front of his statues and why some of his (attributed) sayings are reverently framed and hung on walls.

This does not mean that Westerners have become covert Buddhists. However, it does mean that they have adopted a religious icon to express certain aspects of their own spirituality. Fitness yoga and spa Buddhas fit within a broad undercurrent of spirituality that permeates contemporary American and Western European societies: the spirituality of self-fulfillment. It is a spirituality that is closely linked to the individualism, humanism, and progress-orientedness of the dominant worldviews. The aphorisms of that spirituality are ubiquitous: "believe in yourself," "follow your dreams," "listen to your heart," "find your passion," "live life to the max"—over and over again, they are proclaimed in all sorts of cultural products, from Disney movies to university recruiting leaflets, from self-help books to lifestyle magazines.

Thus, the many forms of spirituality that we find in "secular" societies are not merely a matter of personal questing that allows everyone to develop a unique worldview. They are strongly linked to a much broader and underlying vision of life that pervades all kinds of societal dimensions. In any other context, we would simply regard such a broader and underlying view of life as the dominant religion.

Examples of secular perspectives impairing scientific thinking

As noted in Chapter 5, all scientific research is unavoidably contained within broader ideological frameworks. In secular societies too, scientific research is therefore frequently at odds with reality, regardless of the degree to which people consider themselves to be rational or reasonable. Some of the most infamous examples are the racial theories and eugenics of the nineteenth and twentieth century.

By now, it is more than clear that we cannot divide humanity into different races, but for a long time, the opposite was the dominant scientific consensus. All kinds of attempts were made to develop a racial classification system, and many resources were devoted to extensive research on the matter. As a result, both in the US and in Europe, it was commonplace within several university faculties to classify people into a hierarchy of races on the basis of height, skull shapes, skin colors, eating habits, cultural customs, and so on.

There was, of course, a specific motivation behind this academic obsession with the concept of race. Professor Amade M'charek, who researches the dynamics that still allow racial prejudice to creep into contemporary science, described that motivation very succinctly, when I once interviewed her about this topic:

Philosophers, economists, and biologists were strongly driven by ideals of progress. Intellectuals came together and wondered how they could improve and modernize society.

In their eyes, biology seemed an area in which they could easily intervene. This branch of science could determine which people were allowed to reproduce or not, or which groups should or should not be provided with a better education. In addition, there was the context of colonialism and slavery. When you can organize races hierarchically, you can more easily legitimize why you are allowed to consider some people as your property: they are, so to speak, ranked lower in the evolutionary scale. So, in the end, it was a way of managing and controlling the world.[116]

Many people have difficulty accepting that there once was, and still is, such a thing as "racist science." It does not correspond to the image of science as being wholly neutral and objective, but the fact remains that this racist view of humanity, and the enormous amount of academic research that was linked to its justification, ultimately would form the breeding ground for Nazism and the Shoah (the Holocaust). Unfortunately, many common contemporary ideas about cultural diversity are still tied to concepts that were originally propagated by these racial theories.

In this respect, it is also of importance that Darwin's theories regarding the biological evolution of animal species were incorporated into the racist classifications and eugenics of the early twentieth century. In other words, this great example of a theory which exposes the religious intolerance of rational science, was itself used as an intellectual support for an exceptionally intolerant worldview.

Once again, many examples (including contemporary) could be given, but this specific, and particularly painful, historical example can suffice. It makes the point abundantly clear: "being secular" does not necessarily mean that people are also more open-minded, or that society is construed on a more factual and rationalistic basis.

Examples of secular violence

In the previous chapter, I pointed out how easily we can refer to secular (and at times explicitly atheist) ideologies such as Nazism, Fascism or Stalinist Communism to indicate that a secularized society structure does not necessarily lead to less violence. In recent history, democratic ideals have also lapsed into absolutist violence, resulting in millions of deaths.

The numbers are quite clear in this respect. If we have a look at the ten most violent conflicts of the twentieth century, we can see that not a single one of them arose from major religious motives. Nationalist conflicts in World War I and World War II saw the greatest number of casualties, with more than 40 million and 60 million deaths respectively—far more than any other war in history. Explicitly anti-religious communism also led to several million deaths under the rules of Stalin, Mao and Pol Pot. Numerous civil wars (such as the Russian Civil War, the Biafra War and the contemporary Congolese Civil War) together resulted in some ten million deaths. And finally, there are the many victims of the Cold War, including 2.5 million deaths in the Korean War and 2 million deaths in the Vietnam War, both the result of geopolitical tensions between states that based their policies on capitalist or communist truth claims.[117]

Admittedly, we cannot deny that an enormous amount of violence has been committed on the basis of religious convictions throughout history. However, since the Shoah, the gulags and two atomic bombs, it has become absurd to see religion as *the* source of all violence, since we cannot deny that a great deal of violence has likewise been committed on the basis of secular and "rational" convictions. By now, even the most grotesque and oppressive religiously motivated violence has been more than matched by its secular counterparts.

Of course, all this does not mean that secular societies can be reduced to their violence. Oppression is certainly not their only determining characteristic. It needs little explanation that we should always consider such situations in their entirety. Just as well, it would make little sense to regard secular models of society as *inherently* violent. We should not demonize atheism just because Stalin killed millions of people, nor should we argue that democracy is a problematic form of government because the only country that ever dared to drop two atomic bombs had a democratically elected leadership.

However, if this is so, why are religious societies often scrutinized differently? Even if strong criticism can be voiced about certain forms of oppression, there is no reason why an entire religious tradition should be conflated with that particular aspect. Islamic terrorism certainly was a distressing problem in the early decades of the twenty-first century, but it defines Islam no more than the Shoah defines German culture. The Spanish Inquisition certainly was an example of harsh religious intolerance in the past, but it defines Christianity no more than the 2003 invasion of Iraq defines the American way of life. Religious traditions simply cannot be reduced to their violence. They can only be properly understood when they are considered in their full scope of both positives and negatives.

Examples of the fact that a secular and a religious society do not inherently differ

In some countries it becomes abundantly clear that there is often little difference between religious and secular societies. The United States can serve as prime example. The global economic, political, and military dominance of this country has always been strongly driven by an ideology which political scientists regularly refer to as "American exceptionalism": the notion that the United States is the epitome of freedom and, as such, has the mission to spread and enforce that freedom all over the world.

This notion has seldom been expressed so succinctly as in the words of Herman Melville, the author of the well-known book *Moby-Dick*:

> We Americans are the peculiar, chosen people—the Israel of our time; we bear the ark of the liberties of the world. (...) We are the pioneers of the world; the advance-guard, sent on through the wilderness of untried things, to break a new path in the New World that is ours.[118]

This belief transcends US party leanings and serves as a clear thread throughout their political discourse, as well as in the messages of mainstream media.

In fact, American exceptionalism has a long history. As early as 1630, the idea was articulated by John Winthrop, a leading figure in the first great wave of British migration to North America. While they were still en route in their ship, hoping for a life of happiness in the area that had been recently renamed "New England," he addressed his fellow colonizers with these words:

> The Lord will be our God and delight to dwell among us, as his owne people and will commaund a blessing upon us in all our wayes, soe that wee shall see much more of his wisdome power goodnes and truthe then formerly wee have beene acquainted with, wee shall finde that the God of Israell is among us, when tenn of us shall be able to resist a thousand ot our enemies, when hee shall make us a prayse and glory, that men shall say of succeeding plantacions: the lord make it like that of New England: for wee must Consider that wee shall be as a Citty upon a Hill, the eies of all people are uppon us.[119]

The metaphor of America as a shining city upon a Hill beaming light all over the world, which Winthrop based on verse 5:14 of the Gospel of Matthew, has been quoted several times by various presidents. It was repeated, for example, in speeches by Kennedy, Reagan, and Obama. During the Cold War, the metaphor served as an important symbol representing America as the protector of the free world and democracy. It also permeates the economic vision of many (if not most) political leaders on the republican as well as the democratic side. They do not only see the US as the country chosen to guarantee political freedom, but also as the country that spreads a free market around the world in efforts to increase the happiness of all people.

Of course, the way this underlying ideology is often applied in contemporary geopolitics has been heavily criticized by various groups, both inside and outside the US. After all, the "freedom" that the US officially purports to guarantee meant a protracted war and total destruction for countries such as Vietnam, Afghanistan and Iraq—to name only the best-known conflicts. In addition, the continuing impact of the long history of exterminating Native Americans, enslaving millions of Africans, and racially segregating their society, means that US citizens do not share equally in certain freedoms. Thus, in its real-world political application, the ideology of American exceptionalism often turned out to be merely the ideological justification for violence, oppression, and exploitation for the enrichment of the American elite.

However, the hypocrisy behind this idea of America as an exceptional nation is not the issue here. I merely want to draw attention to its undeniable religious dimension and explore what this implies when it comes to the so-called secularism of the United States. American politicians from all leanings pride themselves on being politicians in a secular country because they hold personal freedom in high esteem. Yet, a quick look at one of the most widely supported underlying ideologies of this secular society has revealed very religious undertones—not least, of course, because American exceptionalism is an obvious continuation of a conviction that originally belonged to an explicitly religious frame of mind.[120]

American exceptionalism is by no means an isolated case. Once we add the concept of "political ideology" to discussions concerning the relationship between religion and secularism, it *always* becomes very difficult to uphold a distinction. Whether we talk about communism, liberalism, capitalism, fascism, or socialism, each of these ideologies is based on beliefs and moral sensitivities; each of them developed hierarchical structures and used strategic violence when they became the guideline of society; and even if some of those ideologies claim to have a purely rational and scientific basis, all of them tout the scientific findings that fit their agenda, while ignoring (and sometimes even actively resisting) the research that undermines it.

This brings us to the end of our overview. The characteristics often attributed to religion appear to apply to secular ideologies and contexts equally often. Hence, we can only conclude that the line between secular and religious approaches toward life is not quite as clear as is often assumed. Differently put, secular and religious societies do not differ all that much.

A brief but necessary note on the separation of church and state

One concept that I have not yet discussed, is the separation of church and state. For many people this element is of crucial importance if we wish to differentiate secular and religious societies. However, this too is less obvious a concept than people might think.

To start with, how can we separate church and state in religious contexts where there is no "church" at all? As I explained in Chapter 2, most major religions have no central hierarchical institution, with some pastoral class on top, determining the correct convictions and proper commandments all adherents should uphold. So, when churchlike institutions are absent from many religious contexts, it makes little sense to try and separate them from the state or vice versa.

One might respond that the crux of the matter is not a literal separation of "church" and "state," but rather that we should approach the concept as a metaphor for something broader: a general separation of religion and politics. In fact, that seems to be the underlying assumption in most public debates concerning this topic. Yet, if this is the case, we end up with even greater conceptual problems: how exactly can we separate the religious from the political when the boundary between them is not clear at all? For example, how will we separate religion and politics in the case of the US, considering the pervasiveness of American exceptionalism? That seems rather impossible.

In contexts driven by other political ideologies, this question does not become easier to address. As I already emphasized, whether we speak of socialism, liberalism, or nationalism, every political ideology portrays all kinds of characteristics normally ascribed to religions. Should they also be separated from politics? That seems a bit absurd.

Let us be honest. No form of politics is free from symbols, rituals, mythologies, ethics and existential first principles. So, the separation of church and state does not offer us a conceptual solution to maintain a clear distinction between a religious and a secular society either.

Why do we not hear a passionate plea for the separation of multinational corporations and state?
There is, of course, a specific context where it does make a lot of sense to talk about the possible need to separate church and state, namely European and American countries where there is indeed a long history

of ecclesiastical institutions which influenced the polity in various ways. Yet, we might wonder why the same principle is rarely applied in other areas. If it is obvious that no single ideological institution should be allowed to monopolize all the political power, then it is perhaps a bit strange we hear so few public debates about the need to curtail the influence of multinational firms. After all, in contemporary European and American contexts, the power of churches is often limited, while the power of extremely hierarchical and wealthy companies is of enormous magnitude. The moral and ideological values they proclaim, such as consumerism and "survival of the richest," are additionally far more dominant and destructive. It therefore seems logical to sometimes be a little less panicky about the separation of church and state, and to be a bit more adamant about the separation of multinational corporations and government.

In this context, it is also particularly interesting that the rise of multinational corporations is directly linked to the emergence of the current view of religion. A good example of this are the scholarships that the East India Company presented to nineteenth-century orientalist academics. The East India Company was a collective of merchants that grew into one of the first multinational corporations in history, and it was instrumental in the British colonization of India. Occasionally the East India Company also paid researchers to extensively map various facets of Indian religions or to translate ancient texts such as the Vedas. The view on religion that developed in the wake of that research—and which still strongly influences our current (mis)conceptions—was therefore largely sponsored by the business world of those days.

In the interlude I already indicated how this view of religion was strongly infused with the racist ideology of the time. The same underlying dynamics that I described there can thus also explain why we do not problematize the very real bond between multinational firms and the state as much as the potential bond between church and state. After all, it is a lot easier to explain the deprivation of large regions of the world by referring to so-called "irrational religious habits" than to be self-reflective and acknowledge the role of economic exploitation.

But how, then, can we make sense of the relationship between religion and secularism? How can we understand the interplay between these concepts when they are not each other's opposites?

We clearly need a different perspective on this subject matter. Let me therefore conclude this chapter with a couple of concrete proposals.

A different look at religion and secularism

Some academic researchers plainly state that religion does not exist. In their view, the distinction between the religious and the secular eventually is not used to indicate that some ideas or customs have specific characteristics or not. Rather, it categorizes *where* those ideas come from and *who* upholds those customs. In that respect, religion and secularism do not actually designate different phenomena, but instead designate the groups they belong to: "we" are secular, while "they" are religious. In other words, the dichotomy between "religious" and "secular" is really nothing more than a veiled distinction between "Western" and "non-Western." At the end of the interlude this was already alluded to.

There is much to be said for this proposition since people often use the binary in such a manner in everyday speech. Without knowing exactly why, most people see the West as secular and the rest of the world as religious. This becomes explicitly noticeable when we consider which ideologies are generally *not* described as a religion, even though they mobilize(d) large groups of people. Nazism, neoliberalism, Stalinist communism and nationalism can once again serve as striking examples. As already explained, they exhibit several features normally associated with religion. All four of them created mythological stories of the world's development and their place within it ("the inherent supremacy of one's race" in Nazism, "the invisible hand of the market" in neoliberalism, "the revolution that liberates us from the evils of capitalism" in Stalinist communism, and "the heroic grandeur of the people" in nationalism); all four have abundant references to foundational scriptures (Hitler's *Mein Kampf* in Nazism, Ayn Rand's *Atlas Shrugged* in neoliberalism, Marx's *Das Kapital* in Stalinist communism, and the constitution of a country in nationalist ideologies); all four are driven by strong beliefs that carry an undeniable moral charge (such as the need for loyalty to the fatherland in Nazism and nationalism, the commitment to the revolution of the proletariat in Stalinist communism, and the desire to get rid of state intervention to "free" the market in neoliberalism); and so on. If such ideologies are not included in books dealing with different world religions, it is not because there are certain characteristics that clearly prevent them from belonging to that category. The only difference between such collectivities and the traditions that are referred to as "world religions" is their origin: if they developed in the modern West, we usually do not call them religious; if they originated elsewhere, we do.

At the beginning of this chapter, it was already indicated that secularism is difficult to define except in direct contrast with religion. From this point of view, it becomes clear why this is the case: that contrast reflects a particular power balance. After all, the word "secular" is not really intended to distinguish between "religious" and "non-religious." It is about a distinction between "the way we modern Westerners think and act" and "the way others think and act."

This approach is supported with thorough arguments by various important scholars of religion.[121] Yet, no matter how far I agree with their reasoning, eventually I do not follow them all the way through because, eventually, it leads to the sheer impossibility to talk about religion. If the words "religious" and "secular" have no meaning in themselves whatsoever, but only make sense as a contrasting pair, then, ultimately, it becomes difficult to straightforwardly categorize commonplace phenomena such as the Christian creed recited during the eucharist, the call to prayer resounding from a mosque, or a puja ritual which is performed in front of a Durga statue. It would become rather absurd if we are no longer able to designate these phenomena as religious (apart from their contrast with something designated as secular).

So, however problematic the contemporary use of the term "religion" might be, when all is said and done, the word does refer to certain concrete realities—but which ones, exactly?

We spontaneously assume that every religion is an amalgam of symbols, rituals, stories, lifestyles and ideas. However, as has become clear from the previous chapters, that amalgam can be quite messy, making it very difficult to determine what exactly constitutes the core of a religion. After all, the various elements of which a religion is composed are dealt with in diverging ways by constituent communities. Some elements are more central than others (such as the figure of Christ in Christianity, the Qur'an in Islam, or the principle of reincarnation in Hinduism), but no single element is the ultimate essence. On top of this, even elements which do occupy a more central position can show a good deal of variation. Over time, core symbols can take on opposing meanings, and the performance of foundational rituals can vary widely from place to place.

When a religion eventually does emerge from the muddle, it is because the various elements are interlinked and group themselves in certain patterns. All kinds of connections are formed between the numerous symbols, rituals, stories, lifestyles, and ideas. So, if we eventually delve deep enough, we will see that the interconnections between some core elements are stronger than others.

Owing to this, I already offered a different conceptualization of religion in Chapter 3. To capture the reality of religion in all its diversity, flexibility, and indefinability, I proposed to use the metaphor of languages. Having arrived at this point of both my deconstruction and reconstruction of the term, I would suggest taking this metaphor quite literally. So, if I eventually must provide an answer to the question "What is religion?" my reply would be: *religions are existential, psychological, and spiritual languages.*

Religions are not languages with words and grammar, but they are languages that, with a plethora of symbols, rituals, stories, lifestyles, and ideas, offer people the possibility to communicate with each other about the existential, psychological, and spiritual elements of life—and the coherence between them.

In fact, such a perspective allows us to include the commonplace descriptions of religion, so the term does not become unusable. Certain elements that are seen as "typically religious," such as the search for the divine, ethical precepts, spiritual teachings, inspired scriptures, and so on, can still be designated as such. Yet, this reframing does allow more room for fluidity and dynamism, compared to the dominant approach. No attempt is made to define the essence of any religion on the basis of a specific list of discrete characteristics— let alone that religion in general is defined by one universally applicable aspect. The fluid interplay between religions and the constant dynamic variation within each religion also becomes included as an inherent part of the phenomenon of religion. Just like languages exchange various elements and morph over time simply because people invariably communicate with one another, religions exchange various elements and morph over time, simply because people will always interact with each other on an existential, psychological, and spiritual level, regardless of their differing backgrounds.

I am fully aware that describing religion as an existential, psychological, and spiritual language does not solve the definitional problems already mentioned in the interlude. All in all, such a description falls somewhere between a functionalist definition of religion (which aims to indicate the role which religion plays in society) and a definition based on family resemblances (which describes religion as a varying constellation of frequently occurring characteristics). Yet, as I explained in the interlude, the problem with these kinds of definitions is that they do not allow us to maintain any meaningful distinction between the religious and the secular.

However, by the end of this chapter, that no longer has to be an issue. We can now simply admit that, if we really observe the world as honestly as possible, every so-called secular society uses a form of existential, psychological, and spiritual language as well. Several examples in this chapter already clarified that major political ideologies such as nationalism, socialism, and liberalism can equally be contained within such a description. We could equally label major sociocultural tendencies such as humanism, fascism, and environmentalism as religious phenomena, since they too form a network of diverse symbols, rituals, stories, lifestyles, and ideas.

As such, it seems better to still retain the concept of "religion," while omitting the concept of "secularism" — or at least the supposed mutual exclusivity between the two. Worldviews and communities that used to be described as "secular" can simply be approached as distinct religious denominations among all others.

The only problem might be that we do not have a name

for the overarching religion to which they belong. In fact, there is a straightforward reason why this is the case: one of the strongest beliefs within that religion is precisely the idea that its adherents are no longer religious. The semi-historical narrative surrounding the heroic attempt to conquer religion and modernize the world became a core part of the mythological narrative of that religion. It is a narrative that is often repeated, telling how the Western world gradually left the dark ages behind and attained enlightenment under the guiding genius of some great scientific thinkers. On top of it, the narrative often adds, this process has not ended yet. We must continue to resist opposing forces and persist in our efforts to spread ever more rational progress all around the world. No matter how abbreviately or elaborately the story is told, we are bound to encounter several typical features of religious myths: a narrative explanation for both the past and the present, a moral signpost for the future, hagiographies of prophetic figures and a symbolism of "light" versus "dark."[122]

Obviously, when people are strongly convinced of such ideas, and when these ideas are deeply entrenched in the social fabric of their society, it becomes very difficult to recognize oneself as religious. Consequently, people who speak this particular religious language will tend to use a conceptual framework with terms such as "secular," "rational," "neutral," and "modern" to describe themselves, while labeling others as "religious," "faithful," "biased," and "traditional" — even if the characteristics they ascribe to "being religious" are equally applicable to "being secular." So, paradoxically enough, the word "secular" is an attempt to distinguish one's own religiosity from all others, and to present it as "the most truthful."

It might of course be possible that I am grossly mistaken and that there is a definite distinction between the religious and the secular. I merely mean to advance a hypothesis. The future will show whether this hypothesis can be upheld.

However, everything else that was explained or proposed in this book is not dependent on the validity of this hypothesis, because even if there would be a distinction between religious and secular ways of life, we can still ask ourselves: what difference does it make? Why is it so important that we are able to delineate that difference? What do we learn from such a distinction? After all, it is *not* the case that religious people, by definition, have a less critical mindset. Neither are they always obliged to abide by specific commandments. (See Chapter 1.) It is *not* the case that religions are, by definition, hierarchically structured, in contrast to the individual freedom of secularity. (See Chapter 2.) It is *not* the case that religious traditions necessarily bind people to a clearly defined religious community, while secular modes of living allow people to deal with the world in a more flexible manner. (See Chapter 3.) It is *not* the case that religions always hamper one's personal spirituality. (See Chapter 4.) It is *not* the case that science only thrives in secular societies. (See Chapter 5.) And above all, it is *not* the case that religious faith, by definition, leads to more violence than secular ideologies. (See Chapter 6.)

So, even if I have overlooked a crucial argument, and secularity does turn out to be something completely different than religiosity, the distinction between the two would still not be significant in the concreteness of everyday life.[123] The fact that someone is religious or secular predicts little to nothing about his or her behavior. In both cases it can lead people in multiple directions. Both a religious and a secular person can have a closed or an open mind; be self-centered or altruistic; live aggressively or peacefully.

In short, even if there was a clear difference between the two, a secular society is not necessarily better than a religious one. Many people might be strongly convinced it is, and this is of course a legitimate position to hold. At the end of the day, however, their view is not based on some long established, self-evident fact. It is not a logical deduction from a more rational view of the world. It is a belief—and often quite a dogmatic one.

In Conclusion

I am fully aware that the message this book hopes to convey might arouse a sense of unease in its readers. The various observations, facts and analyses offered in each chapter strongly conflict with the prevailing views on religion and, as such, they call into question an important part of the dominant, (post) modernist worldview. They destabilize a deeply rooted belief many people uphold.

Yet, as I indicated in the introduction, what this book puts forward does not contradict the findings of contemporary religious studies in any way. There might be some internal academic debates about specific details, but I chose to limit myself as much as possible to elements about which there is a fairly broad consensus. (Excepting, of course, the hypothesis presented in the last chapter that supposedly-secular worldviews are religious as well—though, obviously, I personally see this as the most logical conclusion when taking into account all the facts which were discussed in the previous chapters.) Likewise, the various historical and theological examples that were offered are by no means controversial for those who have studied them. We could add hundreds more which show time and again how diverse, fluid, and permeable religions are.

It is therefore difficult to ignore: our *conceptualization* of religion seems to be at odds with the *reality* of religion. What we think about religion does not correspond to what religion truly is. That is the inevitable conclusion of this book.

Such a conclusion is not only important for discussions among philosophers, theologians, and scholars of religion in the margins of the academic world. It also undermines the vast majority of public debates concerning religion. On a daily basis, we can come across such debates in the media and among politicians. Yet, almost without exception, they are founded upon the disproven seven myths about religion, because these myths are part and parcel of a broader sociopsychological story that portrays our reality as a battle between good and evil. The secular is "good" and "light," whereas the religious is "evil" and "dark."

However, an important nuance must be made. The fact that the basic assumptions about religion are myths rather than facts is not a problem *in itself*. Whatever worldview we hold, to a certain degree, it will *always* be based on myths. That is simply inevitable. After all, we are human beings and not gods, and as such, we are not able to comprehend everything at every instance. We are incapable of achieving a permanent and complete overview of everything which concerns us. That is why humans always were and always will be narrative-based creatures. We cannot but create a story of the many events that determine our lives, the changes in society, and the experiences that affect us in the depths of our being, both personally and collectively. For both our personal life stories and our social myths provide a kind of "summary" to make the enormous tangle of reality somewhat more manageable. Anyone who would want to construct a worldview purely based on facts would soon be faced with an enormous and incomprehensible pile of information. Without perceiving relationships between the facts and without putting them together in a coherent story, they become meaningless.

In this respect too, the description of religion as language is appropriate. Religions are languages which provide meaning. They are languages that allow people to communicate with each other about why some facts and events are more important to them than others. They are languages that make use of symbols, rituals, and mythologies to express deeper truths, which are suspected to be hidden behind the facts, but which cannot always be described literally.

So, when I call today's basic assumptions about religion

"myths," that is not an accusation. All in all, it is simply "the human way" to construct religious stories and myths. However, just like many other aspects of our humanity, they can lead us down different paths: they can open or close our minds; they can strengthen or destroy society; they can create discord or lead to healing.

As such, the fact that the seven basic assumptions about religion are myths is not the crux of the matter. The actual problem is that those specific myths nowadays prevent us from thinking about religion in a solid and sensible manner. At a specific moment in history, the construction of the secularization narrative certainly had valid applicability. Within the context of early modern Europe, it helped a large group of people free themselves from the shackles of ecclesiastical structures and unhealthy power imbalances. Today, however, this story itself is shackling our minds. It hinders a large group of people from accommodating the religious aspects of their lives in a healthy manner because the contemporary (post)modernist view of religion presents a dichotomous and hierarchical worldview that pits people against each other. Not only does it create conflicting categories (such as secular versus religious, Western versus Islamic, Christian versus atheist, and so on), it also presents those categories as core aspects of one's identity, insinuating that they will unavoidably clash—a perfect recipe for a self-fulfilling prophecy.

By giving plenty of examples that dislodge the dominant ideas about religion and by highlighting several historical elements that are too often overlooked, I thus did not simply hope to share some fun facts. Rather, I wanted to offer some concrete possibilities to transcend the sociopolitical tensions surrounding religion, and I hoped to defuse various forms of fundamentalism.

The first form of fundamentalism that I wished to tackle was the fundamentalism of overly dogmatic people who are convinced they must keep their religion as pure as possible and denounce others for doing things differently. In fact, such religious fundamentalists use the same seven myths as their starting point. This can easily be seen when they try to reduce the enormous breadth of their tradition to a list of specific beliefs and commandments; when they present their own tradition as the only one containing any form of truth; and when, for these very reasons, they assume that they are inherently in conflict with people who follow a different tradition.

Hopefully, the contents of the previous chapters can dismantle such a dogmatic view. At the very least, they made it amply clear that, in the end, it is not really feasible to keep a religion "pure." If all traditions over the course of history have become entwined with other traditions, then it simply becomes impossible to distill a "pure" version out of them. I repeatedly emphasized how diverse and fluid all traditions are and, as such, this logically entails that no one can determine once and for all which faction would be the "correct" one among the multitudes.

However, I also wanted to challenge the fundamentalism of some people and groups who portray themselves as secular. Their fundamentalism is at least as problematic in their usage of the seven myths of religion, when stating that they are superior to others; when portraying themselves as "enlightened" and religious people as "underdeveloped"; and when turning their ideas into policy by restricting the religious freedom of others. They too try to preserve the supposed "purity" of their secularism at any cost; they too define their own tradition in an antagonistic and hostile contrast with other traditions; and they too try to impose their truth on others—often by presenting that truth as the only "neutral" and "rational" option.

At the end of this book, I can thus only emphasize that the seven myths about religion deeply hinder our thinking about the collective future of our global society. They keep us stuck in unnecessary tension and discord. If we are to transcend this discord, and the many conflicts it fuels, it is about time religion is freed from the constraints of useless binaries and suffocating purism.

About the author

Jonas Atlas is a Belgian scholar of religion who writes and lectures on the intersection of religion, politics, and mysticism. Though rooted within the Christian tradition, Jonas immersed himself in various other traditions, from Hinduism to Islam. After his studies in philosophy, anthropology, and theology at different universities, he became active in various forms of local and international peace work, often with a focus on cultural and religious diversity.

Jonas currently teaches classes on ethics and spirituality at the KDG University of Applied Sciences and Arts. He is also an independent researcher at the Radboud University, as a member of the Race, Religion, and Secularism network.

His previous books include *Re-visioning Sufism*, which reveals the politics of mysticism behind the contemporary portrayal of Islamic spirituality, and *Halal Monk: A Christian on a Journey through Islam*, which gathered a series of interreligious dialogues with influential scholars, artists, and activists from the Islamic world. The latter won the 2015 Belgian Religious Book of the Year audience award.

Jonas is also the host of (both Dutch and English) podcast series on religion and contemporary spirituality.

You can find an overview of his English publications, listen to his podcasts, and subscribe to his newsletter on www.jonasatlas.net.

Notes

1. See: Pew Research Center, "The Global Religious Landscape," 18.12.2012, http://www.pewforum.org/2012/12/18/global-reli gious-landscape-exec – accessed 01.01.2019.

2. It could of course also be described as a form of pantheism (that is, as a belief that the divine is present in everything), but in this view the divine does not just coincide one-on-one with everything in existence. Even when the entire universe disappears, the One Universal Reality would still remain. Thus, since many Hindus perceive an Eternal Unity behind all reality, it may be more logical to describe it as monotheism or, to be technically correct, as monism.

3. For example, see: Tracy Gordon, "Judaism without God? Yes, say American Atheists," *Religion News Service*, 23.09.2011, https://religionnews.com/2011/09/23/atheist-jews-craft-a-judaism-without-god/ – accessed 11.05.2022; and Pew Research Center, "When Americans Say They Believe in God, What Do They Mean?" 25.04.2018, http://www.pewforum.org/2018/04/25/when-americans-say-they-believe-in-god-what-do-they-mean – accessed 01.01.2019.

4. For example, see: Ellison Banks Findly, *Dana: Giving and Getting in Pali Buddhism*, Motilal Banarsidass, 2003; and Paul Van der Velde, *De oude Boeddha in een nieuwe wereld*, Vantilt, 2015.

5. Although I have so far limited myself to metaphysical components, it is equally impossible to indicate a central belief, common to all religions, in other areas. For example, it seems obvious to question whether there are specific moral convictions that bind all religions together. A good example thereof might be the well-known golden rule: "Treat others as you would like others to treat you." Most certainly, in various expressions this moral guideline can

be found in religious texts from diverse traditions. Yet such a guideline can also be found in ethical frameworks that are not considered to be religious at all. Most atheist humanists will undoubtedly also support such a maxim. So, elements that seem to be present in all religions, are generally found in all kinds of communities, including the non-religious ones. In short, whatever metaphysical, ethical, ritual, or organizational elements we propose, none will be able to serve as the one and only element that unifies all religions. Either those elements will be so specific that they are not present in all religions, or those elements will be so general that they are not unique to religion at all. In the interlude I will return to this conundrum.

6. See: Pew Research Center, "When Americans Say They Believe in God, What Do They Mean?" 25.04.2018, http://www.pewforum.org/2018/04/25/when-americans-say-they-believe-in-god-what-do-they-mean/ – accessed 01.01.2019.

7. See: Klaasjan Baas, "Onderzoek: Nederland is God kwijt geraakt," *Visie*, 2016, https://visie.eo.nl/2016/03/onderzoek-nederland-is-god-kwijt-geraakt/ – accessed 01.03.2019; Ton Bernts and Joantine Berghuijs, *God in Nederland*, Ten Have, 2016.

8. 50:16, M.A.S. Abdel Haleem, *The Qur'an (Oxford World's Classics)*, Oxford University Press, 2005 (2004), Kindle edition. The translation says "him" instead of "you," but this "him" refers to (wo)man in general. I thus took the liberty to change that one word to let the sentence speak for itself without the context of the surrounding verses.

9. 2:115, M.A.S. Abdel Haleem, *The Qur'an (Oxford World's Classics)*, Oxford University Press, 2005 (2004), Kindle edition.

10. See: Meister Eckhart, *Selected Writings*, trans. Oliver Davies, Penguin Books, 1994, pp. 10-11.

11. Claire Gecewicz, "'New Age' beliefs common among both

religious and nonreligious Americans," Pew Research Center, 01.10.2018, http://www.pewresearch.org/fact-tank/2018/10/01 /new-age-beliefs-common-among-both-religious-and-nonreli gious-americans/ – accessed 01.07.2019.

12. See, for example: Rudi Matthee, "Alcohol and Politics in Muslim Culture: Pre-Text, Text and Context," University of Delaware, s.d., https://www.dhi.ac.uk/blogs/intoxicantsproject/wp-con tent/uploads/sites/13/2018/06/6-Matthee-Alcohol-and-Politic s-in-Muslim-Culture.pdf – accessed 27.02.2021.

13. Hafez, *Faces of Love: Hafez and the Poets of Shiraz*, trans. Dick Davis, Penguin Books, 2013 (2012), Kindle edition.

14. Emma Wilby, *Cunning Folk and Familiar Spirits: Shamanistic Visionary Tradition in Early Modern British Witchcraft and Magic*, Sussex Academic Press, 2013 (2005), p. 15.

15. Ibid.

16. People also made a distinction in the types of magic that cunning women used. Some would strongly denounce black magic (that is, magic used to hurt others), while others dared to try it. Consequently, when some of them became the victim of a witch trial, it was not always because they acted as cunning women as such, but rather because they were accused of using their magic *to harm* certain members of the community.

17. Literally the proceedings of her testimony state: "sche answerit, 'That gif sche suld be revin at horis-taillis, sche suld nevir do that.'" (Emma Wilby, *Cunning Folk and Familiar Spirits: Shamanistic Visionary Tradition in Early Modern British Witchcraft and Magic*, Sussex Academic Press, 2013 (2005), p. 12 and p. 96.)

18. Matthew 23:2-3, Holman Bible Staff, *CSB Study Bible*, B&H Publishing Group, 2017, Kindle edition.

19. Matthew 9:13, Holman Bible Staff, *CSB Study Bible*, B&H Publishing Group, 2017, Kindle edition.

20. To make the meaning of the verses as clear as possible for

readers less acquainted with the text, a combination was used of two translations. The first part comes from Lao Tzu, *Tao Te Ching*, trans. D.C. Lau, London: Penguin Books, 1963, p. 45. The last two sentences are from Lao Tzu, *Tao Teh Ching*, trans. John C.H. Wu, New York: Barnes and Noble Books, 1962, p. 77.

21. For an interesting example of a group that went very far in upsetting social norms, we can refer to the followers of the Hindu Kartabhaja. In their cultural context, concepts such as "cleanliness" and "purity" were extremely important. Yet, in order to free themselves from all social attachments and rid their egos of any urge for status or conformism, they chose to blatantly flout those sensibilities. They did this, among other things, by representing the natural elements earth, fire, water, and wind in their tantric rituals with feces, urine, menstrual blood, and semen respectively. See: Jeffrey J. Kripal, *Kali's Child: The Mystical and the Erotic in the Life and Teachings of Ramakrishna*, University of Chicago Press, 1995, p. 290.

22. For example, see: Julius Lipner, *Hindus: Their Religious Beliefs and Practices*, Routledge, 2005 (1994). Even though professor Lipner argues that the Vedas are central to Hinduism (albeit, not so much in their written form and more as an oral tradition), he is quite upfront about the fact that they do not play an important role in the daily religious life of many Hindus: "[I]n practice most Hindus have had no direct access to the Vedas, either in written form or aurally; and (...) for all practical purposes many branches of Hinduism resort to alternative scriptures which seem to have no direct connection with the Vedas." (p. 20) The question whether or not it makes sense to see Hinduism as a religion that is ultimately based on a canon of holy books will be touched upon in the second chapter as well as in the interlude.

23. See, for example, my conversation with Indonesian scholar Musdah Mulia about her interpretation of the Qur'an in relation to human rights and social equality in: Jonas Atlas, *Halal Monk: A Christian on a Journey through Islam*, Yunus Publishing, 2015, p. 214.

24. For example, see: Karen Armstrong, *The Lost Art of Scripture: Rescuing the Sacred Texts*, Knopf, 2019.

25. Origen, *On First Principles*, trans. G.W. Butterworth, Ave Maria Press, 2013, Kindle edition.

26. See: St. Augustine, *The Literal Meaning of Genesis, in Ancient Christian Writers*, vol. 41, trans. John Hammond Taylor, New York: Paulist Press, 1982, http://inters.org/augustine-interpretating-sacred-scripture – accessed 04.11.2019.

27. The first quote is from an informative webpage on the website of the BBC (see: "Hinduism," https://www.bbc.co.uk/religion/religions/hinduism/ataglance/glance.shtml – accessed 21.05.2022), and the second is from the Wikipedia page on Hinduism (see: "Hinduism," https://en.wikipedia.org/wiki/Hinduism – accessed 16.01.2019).

28. J.E. Llewellyn, *Defining Hinduism: A Reader*, Routledge, 2014 (2005), Kindle edition.

29. See for example: Brian K. Pennington, *Was Hinduism Invented? Britons, Indians, and the Colonial Construction of Religion*, Oxford University Press, 2005.

30. Frits Staal, a professor of philosophy, scholar of Hinduism and linguist, once very concisely wrote: "[It is a] known fact that Indian religious traditions emphasize correct practice more than correct doctrine, so that we need the concept of 'orthopraxy' in many contexts where, in the West, 'orthodoxy' would be required. A Hindu may be a theist, pantheist, atheist, communist and believe whatever he likes, but what makes him into a Hindu are the ritual practices he performs and the rules to which he adheres, in short, what he *does*." Frits Staal, *Ritual and Mantras: Rules*

Without Meaning, Motilal Banarsidass, 1996 (Peter Lang Publishing, 1990), p. 389.

31. Once more, see: J.E. Llewellyn, *Defining Hinduism: A Reader*, Routledge, 2014 (2005), Kindle edition.

32. For an example of temples that are managed by low caste groups, see: Timothy Fitzgerald, *The Ideology of Religious Studies*, Oxford University Press, 2000, Kindle edition.

33. Only two examples being Lingayatism, with its estimated ten million adherents in the state of Karnataka, and the International Society of Krishna Consciousness, which spread globally and is better known as the Hare Krishna Movement.

34. In this case "Orthodox" is being used as the common name for one of the three main branches of Christianity. In a way, it is also related to the terminology that was explained in the first chapter since these churches consider themselves to be "followers of the correct teachings," but the term is not generally used in contrast to more orthoprax forms of Christianity. In fact, Orthodox Christianity is, in many respects, much more orthopraxically oriented than, for example, most Protestant denominations.

35. I could also easily add examples from traditions that, in the West, are often less associated with "hierarchy," "centralization" or "dogmatism," such as Buddhism. Take, for instance, Tibetan Buddhism. For centuries the Dalai Lama was not only a religious but also a political leader. I will come back to this later in this chapter. We can also refer to Thai Buddhism. The Thai prince Mongkut founded the Buddhist Dhammayuttika Nikaya movement in 1833. With Mongkut's later crowning as King Rama IV, this Buddhist community became deeply intertwined with the hierarchy of state affairs. Yet, in accordance with everything that was already explained in this chapter, these examples also clarify that Buddhism *as a religion* is

not structured hierarchically. The Dhammayuttika Nikaya has no influence on the Buddhism of the Dalai Lama, and Tibetan Buddhism has no authority over Japanese Zen Buddhism. As such, the fact that all kinds of separate (and very different) hierarchical institutions exist within Buddhism just as well does not imply that Buddhism, as a whole, exhibits a centralist top-down structure.

36. With this concept I inevitably connect with the ideas of Wilfred Cantwell Smith, who already spoke about "cumulative traditions" in his 1962 book *The Meaning and End of Religion*. However, I use the concept in a somewhat different and more limited form myself. Smith tries to use it as a kind of replacement for "religion," whereas I try to indicate a specific facet of the development of religious traditions. Nevertheless, my usage of the term in this book is quite deliberate. As far as I can see, the academic field of religious studies made little use of Smith's concept and as such, by explicitly reappropriating the concept, I hope to indicate that its potential usefulness has been overlooked for too long. (See: Wilfred Cantwell Smith, *The Meaning and End of Religion*, Fortress Press, 1991 (1962).)

37. Only seven percent of the sanctuaries in Europe are dedicated to Jesus. The remaining 27 percent is dedicated to a specific saint. In countries such as Italy, France, Spain, and Belgium, it is even 75 percent of the shrines which are dedicated to Mary. (See: Charlene Spretnak, *Missing Mary*, Palgrave Macmillan, 2004, p. 105. For these percentages, Spretnak herself refers to Mary Lee Nolan and Sidney Nolan, *Christian Pilgrimage in Modern Western Europe*, University of North Carolina Press, 1989, p. 117 and p. 120.)

38. Marina Warner, *Alone of All Her Sex: The Myth and the Cult of the Virgin Mary*, Oxford University Press, 2013 (1976), pp. 312-313.

39. See: Brent Nongbri, *Before Religion: A History of a Modern Concept*, Yale University Press, 2013, Kindle edition.

40. See, for example: Joseph A. Adler, "Chinese Religions: An Overview," in Lindsay Jones (ed.), *Encyclopedia of Religion, 2nd*, Macmillan Reference USA, 2005, https://www2.kenyon.edu/Depts/Religion/Fac/Adler/Writings/Chinese%20Religions%20-%20Overview.htm – accessed 17.08.2019.

41. The *Japan Times* is Japan's largest and oldest English-language newspaper. The quote comes from an article that reported on an exhibition of sacred treasures from Shinto temples at the Tokyo National Museum. The interesting thing about this quote is that this interweaving of Buddhism and Shinto is mentioned very casually and as an obvious matter of fact, indicating how normal it is for Japanese religiosity. See: Sachiko Tamashige, "Seeing Where Shinto and Buddhism Cross," *Japan Times*, 16.05.2013, https://www.japantimes.co.jp/culture/2013/05/16/arts/seeing-where-shinto-and-buddhism-cross/#.XIOK4lNKiu5 – accessed 16.08.2019. For more academic work on such aspects of Japanese religiosity, see, for example: Jason Ananda Josephson, *The Invention of Religion in Japan*, University of Chicago Press, 2012.

42. See: Wendy Doniger, *The Hindus: An Alternative History*, Penguin Press, 2009, Kindle edition. Besides such a ritual overlap between Hindu traditions and Islam, we can also find a lot of ritual overlap with other religions. For example, I once visited a temple where a statue of Jesus had been placed in the classic row of ten incarnations of the god Vishnu, and on the web one can find a very short, but also very interesting documentary, published by the *Wall Street Journal*, about Hindus worshiping Mother Teresa. These Hindus placed her image on their home altars right next to paraphernalia of Shiva, Krishna, and Durga (see:

Why Some in India Worship Mother Teresa as a Goddess, Wall Street Journal, YouTube, 03.09.2016, https://www.youtube.com/watch?v=40rO1im27R8 – accessed 17.08.2019).

Such phenomena are simply common in India. Wendy Doniger once described the situation in India very succinctly as follows: "Nowadays Hindus in India and throughout the diaspora worship the goddess Durga on the days of Durga Puja, Shiva on the nights of Shivaratri, and Ganesha when they begin any new enterprise. Many of them go to church on Christmas eve and worship at the shrines of [Islamic] Sufi pirs from time to time." And that such behavior also applies to Muslims, she clarifies by referring to the Meos, a specific Muslim community from Gurgaon, about which a geographic dictionary from 1911 already wrote that they "keep the feasts of both religions and the fasts of neither." (See: Wendy Doniger, "The Uses and Misuses of Polytheism and Monotheism in Hinduism," https://divinity.uchicago.edu/sites/default/files/imce/pdfs/webforum/012010/monotheism%20for%20religion%20and%20culture-titlecorr.pdf – accessed 01.07.2019.)

43. See: Wendy Doniger, *The Hindus: An Alternative History*, Penguin Press, 2009, p. 548.
44. For example, see: Durre S. Ahmed, "'Real' Men, Naked Women and the Politics of Paradise: The Archetype of Lal Ded," in Durre S. Ahmed (ed.), *Gendering the Spirit: Women and Religion and the Post-Colonial Response*, Zed Books, 2002; Ranjit Hoskote, *I, Lalla: The Poems of Lal Ded*, New Delhi: Penguin Books, 2011, Kindle edition.
45. Wendy Doniger, *The Hindus: An Alternative History*, Penguin Press, 2009, Kindle edition, pp. 532-533.
46. Not to be confused with the famous (and controversial) Indian guru Sathya Sai Baba, who gained popularity not only among Indians but also among many Americans and Europeans in the last decades of the twentieth century. This

Sai Baba was born as Sathyanarayana Raju and claimed to be a reincarnation of Shirdi Sai Baba. However, in a way, he might serve as yet another example in this chapter, since he drew his teachings from various religious traditions and regularly referred to Christianity—not in the least because he, like many other modern Indian gurus of his time, attracted many Westerners.

47. Swami Vivekananda, *Addresses At The Parliament Of Religions*, 1893, https://archive.org/details/AddressesAtTh eParliamentOfReligions – accessed 17.08.2019.

48. M., *The Gospel of Sri Ramakrishna: Originally Recorded by M., a Disciple of the Master*, trans. Swami Nikhilananda, Sri Ramakrishna Math, 1974 (1944). The different parts of the quote are from p. 39 and p. 89.

49. Guru Gobind Singh, *Dasam Granth*, 15.85-16.86, https://www.searchgurbani.com/dasam-granth/page-by-page – accessed 17.08.2019.

50. 2:136, M.A.S. Abdel Haleem, *The Qur'an*, Oxford University Press, Kindle edition. Another example of such a teaching can be found in verse 35:24.

51. Quoted in Brent Nongbri, *Before Religion: A History of a Modern Concept*, Yale University Press, 2013, Kindle edition. For the Arabic version Nongbri himself refers to: C. Eduard Sachau, *Timeline Orientalischer Völker von Alberuni*, F.A. Brockhaus, 1878, p. 207. For the English translation he refers to: Sachau, *The Chronology of Ancient Nations: An English Version of the Arabic Text of the Athar-ul-bakiya of Albiruni*, William II. Allen, 1879, p. 190.

52. Brent Nongbri, *Before Religion: A History of a Modern Concept*, Yale University Press, 2013, Kindle edition.

53. In the Netherlands, for example, research has shown that about a quarter of the population consciously mixes all kinds of elements from different religions or expresses that they feel at home in two or more religions. See: Joantine

Berghuijs, *Meervoudig religieus: Spirituele openheid en creativiteit onder Nederlanders*, Amsterdam University Press, 2018.

54. There is considerable debate about how directly the worship of the goddess Isis influenced the rituals surrounding Mary in the early centuries of Christianity. Some argue that the resemblance between the images of these figures, both referred to as "Mother of God," proves nothing at all and is purely coincidental. Others argue that it is indeed a good example of syncretism. However, a thorough look at all the arguments on both sides convinced me that the arguments weigh in favor of the second group—especially considering everything else which is explained in this chapter. (See, for example: Marianna Delray, "Legacy of the Egyptian Goddess? A Retrospective Look at the Two Divine Mothers, Isis and Mary," s.d., https://www.academia.edu/39877982/legacy_of_the_egyptian_goddess_a_retrospective_look_at_the_two_divine_mothers_isis_and_mary – accessed 15.08.2019.)

    On top of it, even if one doubts the specific relationship between images of Isis and Mary, it is hard to ignore the fact that emerging Christianity was partly taken up by the Greek and Roman populations, because it contained various elements from the popular mystery cults of the time. (See for example: Bart Ehrman, *The Triumph of Christianity*, Simon & Schuster, 2018.)

55. In addition, within a particular tradition there always are several groups that brandish others as "false" or "impure" apostates, and all of those groups are eager to declare themselves the most true or correct expression of their religion. From a historical perspective as well, one group often contradicts the other group, although all of them were convinced they were following the true path. As such, fundamentalists shoot themselves in the foot because,

when one fundamentalist is radically opposed to the other, they both highlight the fact that it is apparently not self-evident to determine which group is right and which is wrong. Hence, the many conflicts among the various fundamentalists are, in themselves, good examples of the fact that the exact boundaries of their religion are not as clear as they would like them to be.

56. Benoît Standaert, *Sharing Sacred Space: Interreligious Dialogue as Spiritual Encounter*, Liturgical Press, 2009, p. 36.

57. Wikipedia, "Religion," https://en.wikipedia.org/wiki/Religion – accessed 29.01.2022.

58. One of the first and most influential pleas in this area was Wilfred Cantwell Smith's book *The Meaning and End of Religion*. As already mentioned in a previous endnote, it appeared already in 1962. It questioned the concept of "religion" and elucidated how this concept clouded our view of what he preferred to refer to as "cumulative traditions." Of course, Smith's proposals also received a lot of criticism—partly because he did not quite succeed in transcending the conceptual problems he raised—but many continued to reflect on the problems he brought to the fore and, with a number of thorough arguments, showed that the contemporary interpretation of "religion" is very dubious to say the least.

For the reflections in this interlude I mainly base myself on the work of Tomoko Masuzawa (*The Invention of World Religions or, How European Universalism was Preserved in the Language of Pluralism*, University of Chicago Press, 2005); William T. Cavanaugh (*The Myth of Religious Violence: Secular Ideology and the Roots of Modern Conflict*, Oxford University Press, 2009); Brent Nongbri (*Before Religion: A History of a Modern Concept*, Yale University Press, 2013); and Peter Harrison (*The Territories of Science and Religion*, University of Chicago Press, 2015). Other interesting and important critical voices in this debate about religion are academics such as Jonathan Z. Smith (for example, *Imagining Religion: From Babylon to Jonestown*, University of Chicago Press, 1982); David Chidester (for example, *Empire of Religion: Imperialism and Comparative Religion*, University of Chicago Press, 2014); Talal Asad (for example, *Genealogies of Religion: Discipline and Reasons of Power in Christianity and Islam*, Johns Hopkins University Press, 1993); Russell T. McCutcheon (for example, *Manufacturing Religion: The Discourse on Sui Generis Religion and the Politics of Nostalgia*, Oxford University Press, 1997); Timothy Fitzgerald (for example, *The Ideology of Religious Studies*, Oxford University Press, 2000); William E. Arnal (for example, *The Sacred is the Profane: The Political Nature of "Religion,"* Oxford University Press, 2013); S.N. Balagangadhara (for example, *"The Heathen in his Blindness..." Asia, the West, and the Dynamic of Religion*, E.J. Brill, 1994); Daniel Dubuisson (for example, *L'Occident et la religion: Mythes, science et idéologie*, Éditions Complexe, 1998); and Eric J. Sharpe (for example, *Comparative Religion: A History*, Duckworth, 1986).

Of course, not all of these academics uphold the same ideas. Whereas some of them would like to replace the concept of "religion" with a more solid term, others would like to drop it altogether; whereas some find the concept problematic because of an inherent lack of analytical power, others mainly criticize its ideological recuperation; whereas some think the word encompasses far too many phenomena, others think the concept is too normative; and so on. However, taken as a whole, their collective research work undeniably shows that the way "religion" is mostly used as an analytical category actually does not make the world more comprehensible, but rather sows confusion and, as I will explain further in this chapter, is strongly intertwined with specific political power relations.

59. For the fact that the concept of "religion" did not exist in ancient China, see for example: Joseph A. Adler, "Chinese Religions: An Overview," in: Lindsay Jones (ed.), *Encyclopedia of Religion*, Macmillan Reference USA, 2005, https://www2.kenyon.edu/Depts/Religion/Fac/Adler/Writings/Chinese%20Religions%20-%20Overview.htm – accessed 17.08.2019. For the fact that it also was not present in ancient Japan, see for example: Jason Ananda Josephson, *The Invention of Religion in Japan*, University of Chicago Press, 2012. For the fact that the word just as well did not exist in North American traditions, see for example: Tink Tinker, "Irrelevance of Euro-Christian Dichotomies for Indigenous Peoples: Beyond Nonviolence to a Vision of Cosmic Balance," in: Irfan Omar & Michael Duffey (eds.), *Peacemaking and the Challenge of Violence in World Religions*, Wiley-Blackwell, 2015, pp. 206-229. And for the fact that religion was absent from the languages of pre-colonial India (and a variety of other contexts), see for example: Wilfred Cantwell Smith, *The Meaning and End of Religion*, Fortress Press, 1991 (1962), and Brent Nongbri, *Before Religion: A History of a Modern Concept*, Yale University Press, 2013.

60. For example, see: Bart Ehrman, *The Triumph of Christianity*, Simon & Schuster, 2018; S.N. Balagangadhara, *"The Heathen in his Blindness…" Asia, the West, and the Dynamic of Religion*, E.J. Brill, 1994.

61. Related to all of this is the interesting fact that, for centuries, European intellectuals were convinced that Islam was actually a heretical form of Christianity and therefore not a separate religion. "In the eighth century, the Christian monk John of Damascus set a lasting precedent by classifying followers of Muhammad not as members of a separate religion but as Christian heretics. Although it may seem odd from a modern standpoint to classify Muslims as Christians, this mode of classification (…) [and] the

193

notion that Muhammad had a heretical Christian teacher would persist for centuries among Christians." (Brent Nongbri, *Before Religion: A History of a Modern Concept*, Yale University Press, 2013, Kindle edition.)

62. William T. Cavanaugh, *The Myth of Religious Violence: Secular Ideology and the Roots of Modern Conflict*, Oxford University Press, 2009, Kindle edition.

63. For example, of the missionaries in India, see: S.N. Balagangadhara, *"The Heathen in his Blindness..."* Asia, the West, and the Dynamic of Religion, E.J. Brill, 1994. For examples of the Khoikhoi, see: David Chidester, *Savage Systems: Colonialism and Comparative Religion in Southern Africa*, University Press of Virginia, 1996.

64. William T. Cavanaugh, *The Myth of Religious Violence: Secular Ideology and the Roots of Modern Conflict*, New York: Oxford University Press, 2009, Kindle edition.

65. Some important scholars were listed in the second note of this chapter.

66. F. Max Müller, *Introduction to the Science of Religion: Four Lectures Delivered at the Royal Institution With Two Essays On False Analogies and the Philosophy of Mythology*, Longmans, Green, and Co., 1873, pp. 122-123.

67. There is, of course, a certain element of irony in all of this. As I mentioned in Chapter 1, whether or not Buddhism is a religion is a contested topic today. Western Buddhists often say they feel drawn to that particular tradition exactly because, in their view, it is *not* a religion. Yet, historically speaking, it was the first tradition to be considered a real rival to Christianity because, unlike other traditions, it was a border-crossing religion.

68. This view was quite common among academics with Protestant backgrounds. Because of their own religious views on the Bible, they placed particular emphasis on the centrality of sacred scriptures. Even though some

traditions were strongly orthoprax, they invariably looked for ancient texts, which they could place within a canon of "holy books." They then defined the essence of those traditions mainly on the basis of those texts and books. Brent Nongbri summarized this dynamic very succinctly in his book *Before Religion*: "As scholars wrote about the religious systems they detected in these ancient texts, they generated pure, textual religions that provided a standard by which Europeans could judge (and often condemn) the practices of modern peoples as not being true to these ancient 'authentic' religions. This opinion held not only for Hinduism, but for all of the 'Oriental religions.'" (Brent Nongbri, *Before Religion: A History of a Modern Concept*, Yale University Press, 2013, Kindle edition.)

69. Jonathan Z. Smith, "Religion, Religions, Religious," in Mark C. Taylor (ed.), *Critical Terms for Religious Studies*, University of Chicago Press, 1998, p. 280.

70. According to a 2017 survey by the Pew Research Forum, 27 percent of the US population agree with the label of "spiritual but not religious." (See: Michael Lipka and Claire Gecewicz, "More Americans Now Say They're Spiritual but Not Religious," Pew Research Center, 06.09.2017, https://www.pewresearch.org/fact-tank/2017/09/06/more-americans-now-say-theyre-spiritual-but-not-religious/ – accessed 17.08.2019.) In fact, another US survey of 1,200 adolescents found that 72 percent of those born around the turn of the millennium self-describe that way. (See: Cathy Lynn Grossman, "Survey: 72% of Millennials 'More Spiritual than Religious,'" *USA Today*, 27.04.2010, https://usatoday30.usatoday.com/news/religion/2010-04-27-1Amillfaith27_ST_N.htm – accessed 17.08.2019.) In Canada, 39 percent confirm the statement, according to a 2015 study by the Agnus Reid Institute. (See: Angus Reid Institute, "Religion and faith in Canada today: strong

belief, ambivalence and rejection define our views," 26.03.2015, http://angusreid.org/faith-in-canada/2015 – accessed 17.08.2019.) In a country like the Netherlands, only ten percent of those who do not feel affiliated with a particular religious tradition would describe themselves as spiritual. However, research by the Free University of Amsterdam, which mentions the statistic, also shows that 28 percent of the Dutch can be referred to as "somethingist" (i.e., as a person who believes in a difficult to define higher power, but not necessarily in the type of God described by the larger religious traditions). It seems realistic therefore to suppose that the term "spiritual" is not interpreted in the same way by everyone in the Netherlands. If we classify "somethingists" as "spiritual but not religious" based on the content of their views, we arrive at corresponding percentages. (See: Klaasjan Baas, "Onderzoek: Nederland is God kwijt geraakt," *Visie*, 2016, https://visie.eo.nl/2016/03/onderzoek-nederland-is-god-kwijt-geraakt/ – accessed 01.03.2019. See also: Ton Bernts and Joantine Berghuijs, *God in Nederland*, Ten Have, 2016.) Accordingly, a European Commission survey shows that in France, 27 percent of the population believes "there is some spirit or life force" rather than "there is a God" or "there is no God." (See: TNS Opinion & Social, *Eurobarometer on Biotechnology*, Special Eurobarometer (341), European Commission, 10.2010, p. 381, http://ec.europa.eu/commfrontoffice/publicopinion/archives/ebs/ebs_341_en.pdf – accessed 17.08.2019.)

71. See: Jonas Atlas, *Re-visioning Sufism*, Yunus Publishing, 2019. Readers who have a need for more examples and a more thorough exposition of this subject are referred to this publication.

72. Tomoko Masuzawa, *The Invention of World Religions or, How European Universalism was Preserved in the Language of*

Pluralism, University of Chicago Press, 2005, p. 26.

73. The Hasidic community is, of course, by no means the only example of Jewish spirituality and mysticism. There are many other examples of different factions and communities, some more orthodox than others, and some more orthoprax than others. Thus, the Baal Shem Tov did not conjure up his ideas out of thin air. He based himself on dimensions of Judaism that we can easily trace back to the time when Jesus preached. See for example: Gerard F. Willems, *Jezus en de chassidim van zijn dagen: een godsdiensthistorische ontdekking*, Ten Have, 1996.

74. In the Hindu traditions and the various religious classics that discuss the term, "yoga" can denote various forms of spiritual connection. I have restricted myself to the most common meanings still utilized today. For those who would like an overview of all possible meanings that the word "yoga" has been given in different texts, see: James Mallinson, *Roots of Yoga*, Penguin Classics, 2017.

75. In fact, the Sanskrit word *"asana"* originally meant "sitting posture." Only later did it receive the more general meaning of "bodily posture" (Arthur Anthony MacDonell, *A Practical Sanskrit Dictionary*, University of Chicago, 2005 (1929), https://dsalsrv04.uchicago.edu/cgi-bin/app/macdonell_query.py?=%E0%A4%86%E0%A4%B8%E0%A4%A8&searchhws=yes – accessed 17.01.2019). One can see this in the *Yoga Sutras* of Patanjali, which are often regarded as the classic scriptural reference of yoga practice. The first two sentences of the sutras are: "And now the teaching of yoga begins. Yoga is the settling of the mind in silence." A little further, it reads: "There are five types of mental activity. They may or may not cause suffering. These five are: understanding, misunderstanding, imagination, sleep and memory. (…) These five types of mental activity are settled through the practice of yoga and the freedom it bestows. The practice

of yoga is the commitment to become established in a state of freedom." *Asanas* (postures) are not discussed until the second chapter. They are described as one of the eight "limbs" or stages in a fairly classical yoga scheme, which also includes "moral behavior," "proper breathing" and "concentration." Bodily postures are mentioned only once more: "The physical postures should be steady and comfortable. They are mastered when all effort is relaxed and the mind is absorbed in the Infinite. Then we are no longer upset by the play of opposites." All in all, these verses merely mention a preparation for the actual meditation. (Translations taken from *The Yoga Sutras of Patañjali*, translated and introduced by Alistair Shearer, Rider, 2002 (1982), p. 90 & pp. 110-111.)

76. Mark Singleton, *Yoga Body: The Origins of Modern Posture Practice*, Oxford University Press, 2010, Kindle edition.

77. See: Mark Singleton, *Yoga Body: The Origins of Modern Posture Practice*, Oxford University Press, 2010, Kindle edition; Elliott Goldberg, *The Path of Modern Yoga: The History of an Embodied Spiritual Practice*, Inner Traditions, 2016.

78. Most certainly, we could identify many other important influences on the spiritual interpretation of contemporary yoga that originated in the West. For example, the widespread Theosophy disseminated a strong occultist (and orientalist) interpretation of some Hindu concepts to a broad Western audience, but I will stick to this one particular example of early twentieth century New Thought spirituality because of its direct connection with physical culture.

79. William C. Chittick (ed.), *The Essential Seyyed Hossein Nasr*, World Wisdom, 2007, Kindle edition.

80. Early protagonists of this philosophical movement were René Guénon, Ananda Coomaraswamy and Frithjof

Schuon. In addition to Nasr, people such as Titus Burckhardt, Martin Lings, Jean-Louis Michon and Huston Smith were key figures of the second-generation.

81. In this context, words like "esoteric" or "esotericism" should not be confused with the contemporary use of those words which often carry the connotation of "occult" and "mysterious."

82. I once came across a good example of this at a 5Rhythms Dance session. An altar was erected in the dance hall, with a statue of the Buddha prominently placed on top of it. A few candles had been placed in front of the statue and behind the altar hung a piece of cloth portraying the silhouette of a yogi, showing the different chakras. Nevertheless, the 5Rhythms Dance is not a form of Buddhism or Hinduism. It is a very open form of dance in which there are no fixed dance steps and everyone is free to move as he or she wishes. In accordance with the name, the structure of the dance session is mainly determined by five types of music that, taken together, form a "wave": flowing introductory music, somewhat firmer staccato, exuberant chaos, lyrical cooling down and silence.

This 5Rhythms Dance form was originally invented by Gabrielle Roth and was never merely intended as a kind of workout. From the outset it was associated with spiritual psychotherapy. (This is also evident from the fact that Roth taught at *The Kripalu Center for Yoga & Health* and the *Omega Institute for Holistic Studies*.) The facilitator in the session I attended also repeatedly advised to "let your heart speak through your dance" and to "ground yourself." During a brief moment of explanation in between two waves of music, he also referred to shamanism and yoga.

Thus, at first glance, the 5Rhythms Dance might seem like a perfect example of a gathering that is spiritual but not religious. Yet, that raises the question how we should interpret the explicit references to religious traditions. Perhaps it is better to speak of multiple religious belonging, as explained in Chapter 3, since the 5Rhythms Dance itself contains all kinds of religious elements: its "teaching" goes back to a specific founder (and many facilitators claim greater authority when they can demonstrate a direct master-disciple relationship with Gabrielle Roth); the standard structure of the sessions provides a clear ritual dimension; the majority of the dancers seem to agree with a specific worldview (which can be easily traced to the founder's vision); and during the ritual, specific rules of conduct are observed (such as not talking, not using any drugs and dancing barefoot). So, on the basis of the prevailing view of religion, the label "religious" seems rather appropriate for 5Rhythms Dance. It certainly does not seem any less religious than, for instance, a kecak trance dance in Indonesia, an ecstatic zikr in Chechnya or a traditional rain dance among Native Americans.

83. A few examples are Philip Clayton and Zachary Simpson (eds.), *The Oxford Handbook of Religion and Science*, Oxford University Press, 2006; George Saliba, *Islamic Science and the Making of the European Renaissance*, MIT Press, 2007; James Hannam, *God's Philosophers: How the Medieval World Laid the Foundations of Modern Science*, Icon Books, 2009; Peter Harrison (ed.), *The Cambridge Companion to Science and Religion*, Cambridge University Press, 2010; John Hedley Brooke & Ronald L. Numbers (eds.), *Science and Religion Around the World*, Oxford University Press, 2011; Peter Harrison, *The Territories of Science and Religion*, University of Chicago Press, 2015. In this chapter I mainly base myself on these books as well.

84. Quoted in James Hannam, *God's Philosophers: How the Medieval World Laid the Foundations of Modern Science*, Icon Books, 2009, Kindle edition.

85. For a more thorough discussion of both Galileo's trial and the controversy surrounding Copernicus, see: James Hannam, *God's Philosophers: How the Medieval World Laid the Foundations of Modern Science*, Icon Books, 2009. The same book also delves deeper into the life and work of Johannes Kepler, who provided the final conclusive proof of heliocentrism by no longer assuming that planets revolve around the sun in circles and by proposing they had elliptical trajectories. His books did not generate any controversy or censorship from the Church, but his ideas did not become well established until the seventeenth century, because, as James Hannam writes, "publicising his ideas was not Kepler's strongest point. He wrote voluminous tomes but they are practically unreadable. His laws are not hard to explain but you would never guess this from his convoluted explanations. Part of the trouble was with Kepler's religion. He saw his science as a religious duty and wrote as if it was a complicated piece of theology. His notebooks are even worse. Sheet after sheet of calculations are punctuated with mystical speculation and prayers."

86. Peter Harrison, *The Territories of Science and Religion*, University of Chicago Press, 2015, Kindle edition.

87. Ibid.

88. Ibid.

89. Ibid.

90. We should also keep in mind that the debate surrounding Darwin's theory of evolution was by no means merely a matter of accepting or rejecting scientific facts. It was also part of an important moral discussion. As Professor John Hedley Brooke writes: "There are many reasons why Darwinism in America developed a high public profile. It was drawn into discussions about race when, in the 1860s, the Civil War elevated the issue, and well into the twentieth century, it was also invoked to support highly

controversial eugenic proposals. (…) The question of racial improvement was addressed in many eugenic proposals during the late nineteenth and early twentieth centuries. (…) The association of Darwinism with eugenics was strong in Britain, represented by the geneticist Ronald Fisher (1890-1962) for whom it was a practical Christian duty to encourage breeding among those of 'higher ability, richer health, and greater beauty.' American evangelicals, many suspicious of attempts at racial engineering, were apt to see Darwinism as villain and partner in crime." (John Hedley Brooke, "Modern Christianity," in: John Hedley Brooke and Ronald L. Numbers (eds.), *Science and Religion Around the World*, Oxford University Press, 2011, pp. 109-110.) Today, therefore, many would argue that on this specific moral point, the Evangelicals of the time were on the right side of history in contrast to the racist eugenicists who supported the theory of evolution. I will come back to this in Chapter 7.

91. Jon H. Roberts, "Religious reactions to Darwin," in: Peter Harrison (ed.), *The Cambridge Companion to Science and Religion*, Cambridge University Press, 2010, pp. 82-83.

92. I base myself on statistics that were collected by the Pew Research Center. (See: David Masci, "For Darwin Day, 6 facts about the evolution debate," Pew Research Center, 11.02.2019, https://www.pewresearch.org/fact-tank/2019/02/11/darwin-day/ – accessed 17.08.2019; Cary Funk, "How highly religious Americans view evolution depends on how they're asked about it," Pew Research Center, 06.02.2019, https://www.pewresearch.org/fact-tank/2019/02/06/how-highly-religious-americans-view-evolution-depends-on-how-theyre-asked-about-it/ – accessed 09.05.2022.) These figures present significantly less rejection of the theory of evolution in comparison to previous years since they discovered the way the question

was phrased greatly influenced the answers. This is explained more thoroughly at the end of this chapter.

93. See: Geoffrey Cantor, "Modern Judaism," in John Hedley Brooke and Ronald L. Numbers (eds.), *Science and Religion Around the World*, Oxford University Press, 2011, pp. 50-62.

94. For example, see: Marwa Elshakry, *Reading Darwin in Arabic, 1860-1950*, University of Chicago Press, 2014, p. 137.

95. George Saliba, *Islamic Science and the Making of the European Renaissance*, MIT Press, 2007, Kindle edition.

96. For example, in an essay on science in Chinese traditions, sinologist Mark Csikszentmihalyi writes: "The history of natural philosophy and the early history of Chinese religions are just as intertwined as they are in ancient cultures throughout the world, which is to say that there was no formal division between the two." (Mark Csikszentmihalyi, "Early Chinese Religions," in: John Hedley Brooke and Ronald L. Numbers (eds.), *Science and Religion Around the World*, Oxford University Press, 2011, p. 175.) And historian of science John Hedley Brooke is just as straightforward when he elaborates on the period in Indian history in which the Western image of religion and science was introduced through colonization: "Despite the existence of conservative reform movements in India, which reaffirmed the authority of the sacred Vedic texts, and despite some antagonism to Christianity that found expression under British rule, [...] traditional almanacs continued to be produced even while serious astronomical research was conducted at the Madras Observatory. Even the potential threat to religious values posed by Charles Darwin's theory of evolution rarely materialized in India because what mattered in prevalent forms of the religious life was the cultivation of an inner spiritual evolution, a goal largely untouched by Darwin's case for the material

derivation of species from their progenitors." (John Hedley Brooke and Ronald L. Numbers (eds.), *Science and Religion Around the World*, Oxford University Press, 2011, p. 8.)

97. Peter Harrison (ed.), *The Cambridge Companion to Science and Religion*, Cambridge University Press, 2010, p. 4.

98. See: Cary Funk, "How highly religious Americans view evolution depends on how they're asked about it," Pew Research Center, 06.02.2019, https://www.pewresearch. org/fact-tank/2019/02/06/how-highly-religious-americans-view-evolution-depends-on-how-theyre-asked-about-it/ – accessed 09.05.2022.

99. Because of this, the most adamant supporters of the scientific method sometimes made ideological mistakes. An ironic example can be found in the writings of Karl Popper, the influential philosopher of science who introduced the concept of "falsification" around the middle of the twentieth century and thus formulated a basic principle of the contemporary scientific method. In one of his last essays, he wrote: "[The scientific method] seems to have been invented only once in human history [in the Ionian school of Thales]. It died in the West when the schools in Athens were suppressed by a victorious and intolerant Christianity, though it lingered in the Arab East. In the renaissance it was not so much reinvented as reimported from the East, together with the rediscovery of Greek philosophy and Greek science. (...) Human science started from a bold and hopeful attempt to understand critically the world in which we live. This ancient dream found fulfilment in Newton. We can say that only since Newton humanity became fully conscious—conscious of its position in the universe." (Karl R. Popper, *The Myth of the Framework: In Defense of Science and Rationality*, Routledge, 1994, p. 42.) As may be clear from what was already explained in this chapter and what has been explained in

the side note about the scientific approach of the ancient Greeks, as good as everything in this quote is problematic from a historical perspective. Nevertheless, because of his ideological assumptions, this famous proponent of the scientific method could make his claim without much reservation.

100. See, for example: Elaine Howard Ecklund and Christopher P. Scheitle, *Religion vs. Science: What Religious People Really Think*, Oxford University Press, 2018, Kindle edition. While this book focuses solely on the situation in the US, it is the largest study ever conducted on the topic. The results of the study are based on a representative survey that surveyed more than 10,000 Americans and 320 in-depth interviews with people from 23 different faith communities. Moreover, the social debates about religion and science in the US are more polarized, making the findings from such a context even more interesting. In the introduction to their book, the researchers do not mince words: "Jews, Muslims, and most Christians, for example, show similar or higher levels of interest in science than do nonreligious Americans. Our national survey shows that evangelicals have slightly lower interest levels in science, but this does not mean that they are hostile to science. For instance, when we asked survey respondents if they thought that, 'overall, modern science does more harm than good,' evangelicals were just as likely to disagree with this statement as anyone else." Many other findings from the study confirm that the vast majority of American citizens, who see themselves as members of a religious community, experience no conflict whatsoever between religion and science.

101. William T. Cavanaugh, *The Myth of Religious Violence: Secular Ideology and the Roots of Modern Conflict*, Oxford University Press, 2009, Kindle edition, p. 164 and p. 163.

102. Ibid., p. 155.

103. John Bossy, *Christianity in the West, 1400-1700*, Oxford University Press, 1985, p. 153.
104. The death toll is a frequently proposed average of the most common estimates, but, as Ian Talbot and Gurharpal Singh suggest, those estimates can vary greatly: "The death toll remains disputed with figures ranging from 200,000 to 2 million." (Ian Talbot and Gurharpal Singh, *The Partition of India*, Cambridge University Press, 2009, p. 2.)
105. Mohandas Karamchand Gandhi, *An Autobiography or The Story of My Experiments with Truth*, Penguin Books, 2001 (1927), p. 14.
106. Mohandas Karamchand Gandhi, "Speech at Prayer Meeting – 12.01.1948," in: *Collected Works of Mahatma Gandhi*, vol. 98, Publications Division Government of India, 1999, p. 220, https://www.gandhiashramsevagram.org/gandhi-literature/collected-works-of-mahatma-gandhi-volume-1-to-98.php
107. Clayborne Carson, Susan Carson, Adrienne Clay, Virginia Shadron, and Kieran Taylor (eds.), *The Papers of Martin Luther King, Jr., Volume IV: Symbol of the Movement, January 1957–December 1958*, University of California Press, 2000, p. 478.
108. Martin Luther King, "I Have a Dream," Washington DC, 28.08.1963, https://americanrhetoric.com/speeches/mlkihaveadream.htm – accessed 17.08.2018.
109. For example, see: Paul Moses, *The Saint and the Sultan: The Crusades, Islam, and Francis of Assisi's Mission of Peace*, Doubleday Religion, 2009; and Jan Hoeberichts, *Franciscus en de sultan: mannen van vrede*, Valkhof pers, 2012.
110. Chomsky & Herman, *Manufacturing Consent: The Political Economy of the Mass Media*, Vintage digital, 2008 (1988), Kindle edition.
111. For example, see: David Fromkin and James Chace, "Vietnam: The Retrospect: What Are the Lessons of

Vietnam?" in: *Foreign Affairs*, spring 1985, https://www. foreignaffairs.com/articles/vietnam/1985-03-01/vietnam-retrospect-what-are-lessons-vietnam

112. Chomsky & Herman, *Manufacturing Consent: The Political Economy of the Mass Media*, Vintage digital, 2008 (1988), Kindle edition.

113. Human Rights Watch, "Egypt: Year of Abuses Under al-Sisi," 2015.

114. Michael R. Gordon and Kareem Fahim, "Kerry Says Egypt's Military Was 'Restoring Democracy' in Ousting Morsi," *New York Times*, 01.08.2013, http://www.nytimes. com/2013/08/02/world/middleeast/egypt-warns-morsi-supporters-to-end-protests.html?_r=0 – accessed 17.08.2019.

115. Concerning the religious "magic" of that last example, David Graeber, a professor of economic anthropology, succinctly wrote: "These days, it's hard to recall the almost mystical aura with which the financial sector had surrounded itself in the years leading up to [the worldwide financial crash of] 2008. Financiers had managed to convince the public—and not just the public, but social theorists too (I well remember this)—that with instruments such as collateralized debt obligations and high-speed trading algorithms so complex they could be understood only by astrophysicists, they had, like modern alchemists, learned ways to whisk value out of nothing by means that others dared not even try to understand." People with a more materialistic worldview often argue that the magical thinking, which is a part of certain religious contexts, is complete nonsense and generally used to fool gullible people. Rarely someone remarks that this type of magical thinking equally applies to completely different contexts, such as the financial sector. Graeber's example makes this quite clear, however, as he himself adds: "Then, of

course, came the crash, and it turned out that most of the instruments were scams. Many weren't even particularly sophisticated scams." (David Graeber, *Bullshit Jobs: A Theory*, Simon & Schuster, 2018, Kindle edition.)

116. Jonas Slaats, "De wetenschap van ras en het racisme van de wetenschap," *Kif Kif*, 25.01.2019, https://kifkif.be/cnt/artikel/de-wetenschap-van-ras-en-het-racisme-van-de-wetenschap-7041 – accessed 17.08.2019. My translation into English.

117. The numbers are averages of the lowest and highest estimations by various historians, taken from Wikipedia, "List of wars by death toll," https://en.wikipedia.org/wiki/List_of_wars_by_death_toll and Wikipedia, "List of wars and anthropogenic disasters by death toll," https://en.wikipedia.org/wiki/List_of_wars_and_anthropogenic_disasters_by_death_toll. Both accessed 01.08.2015.

118. Herman Melville, *White Jacket or, the World on a Man-of-War*, The Floating Press, 2010 (1850), p. 202.

119. John Winthrop, "City upon a Hill," 1630, http://www.digitalhistory.uh.edu/disp_textbook.cfm?smtID=3&psid=3918 – accessed 17.08.2019.

120. For those who would like to delve deeper into the theology and religiosity of American exceptionalism, I refer to Professor William Cavanaugh's extensive analysis in his book *Migrations of the Holy*. Much of what I describe here is also inspired by or based on this book. See: William T. Cavanaugh, *Migrations of the Holy: God, State, and the Political Meaning of the Church*, William B. Eerdmans, 2011.

121. In an endnote of the interlude, I already mentioned a few names, such as Wilfred Cantwell Smith, Jonathan Z. Smith, David Chidester, Tomoko Masuzawa, Brent Nongbri, Russell McCutcheon, William Arnal and Timothy Fitzgerald. Their research work shows in various ways that the distinction between secular and religious is largely a

matter of a deeper duality between Western and non-Western, which builds on colonial ideas. Some of them even come to the conclusion that we should completely abolish the word "religion."

122. Of course, in line with the idea that no single element determines any religious tradition, it is not my intention to imply that this particular narrative and mythology would be upheld by all adherents of this religion-without-a-name. It is simply a set of beliefs which are quite dominant, and which can be encountered in different ideological constellations.

123. For example, one option I did not discuss was articulated by the influential philosopher Charles Taylor. In his well-known book *A Secular Age* he describes the difference between a secular and a religious world mainly as a matter of existential optionality: "[I]n our western civilization[, we] have changed not just from a condition where most people lived 'naïvely' in a construal (part Christian, part related to 'spirits' of pagan origin) as simple reality, to one in which almost no one is capable of this, but all see their option as one among many. We all learn to navigate between two standpoints: an 'engaged' one in which we live as best we can the reality our standpoint opens us to; and a 'disengaged' one in which we are able to see ourselves as occupying one standpoint among a range of possible ones, with which we have in various ways to coexist." (Charles Taylor, *A Secular Age*, The Belknap Press of Harvard University Press, 2007, p. 12.) So, according to Taylor, the fact that we can choose whether or not to believe in God or adhere to certain truth claims provides the crucial distinction. In religious contexts, a specific religious worldview would be a social fact, while in a secular world there would be a choice of differing positions. However, there are two reasons why I do not discuss this view.

First of all, there is a logical inconsistency: the difference supposedly lies in the ability to choose, but if that is the case, then secularism itself would not be a choice. The view that all religions are subordinate to an overarching secular worldview is just as much a social fact as religions were before. In addition, Taylor's proposal also too easily ignores the enormous diversity that has always existed within all religious worldviews. As the many examples from the previous chapters show, religions are by no means always and everywhere a mental and moral straitjacket within which only one vision and way of life are possible. Every religion encompasses all kinds of tendencies, currents and schools of thought that are sometimes diametrically opposed to one another. In the past, religious people were therefore faced with all kinds of choices, and they partly also took a "disengaged" position.

Above all, however, the same basic point also applies here: even if Taylor's vision were to indicate an essential difference, it still does not matter all that much in terms of the actual sociopolitical dynamics within a society. For even if "a secular age" were to allow individuals a greater existential optionality, that age is no less violent, no less hierarchical, no more scientific, and so on.

ACADEMIC AND SPECIALIST

Iff Books publishes non-fiction. It aims to work with authors and titles that augment our understanding of the human condition, society and civilisation, and the world or universe in which we live.
If you have enjoyed this book, why not tell other readers by posting a review on your preferred book site.
Recent bestsellers from Iff Books are:

Why Materialism Is Baloney
How true skeptics know there is no death and fathom answers to life, the universe, and everything
Bernardo Kastrup
A hard-nosed, logical, and skeptic non-materialist metaphysics, according to which the body is in mind, not mind in the body.
Paperback: 978-1-78279-362-5 ebook: 978-1-78279-361-8

The Fall
Steve Taylor
The Fall discusses human achievement versus the issues of war, patriarchy and social inequality.
Paperback: 978-1-78535-804-3 ebook: 978-1-78535-805-0

Brief Peeks Beyond
Critical essays on metaphysics, neuroscience, free will, skepticism and culture
Bernardo Kastrup
An incisive, original, compelling alternative to current mainstream cultural views and assumptions.
Paperback: 978-1-78535-018-4 ebook: 978-1-78535-019-1

Framespotting
Changing how you look at things changes how
you see them
Laurence & Alison Matthews
A punchy, upbeat guide to framespotting. Spot deceptions and
hidden assumptions; swap growth for growing up. See and be free.
Paperback: 978-1-78279-689-3 ebook: 978-1-78279-822-4

Is There an Afterlife?
David Fontana
Is there an Afterlife? If so what is it like? How do Western ideas
of the afterlife compare with Eastern? David Fontana presents the
historical and contemporary evidence for survival of
physical death.
Paperback: 978-1-90381-690-5

Nothing Matters
a book about nothing
Ronald Green
Thinking about Nothing opens the world to everything by
illuminating new angles to old problems and stimulating new
ways of thinking.
Paperback: 978-1-84694-707-0 ebook: 978-1-78099-016-3

Panpsychism
The Philosophy of the Sensuous Cosmos
Peter Ells
Are free will and mind chimeras? This book, anti-materialistic but
respecting science, answers: No! Mind is foundational
to all existence.
Paperback: 978-1-84694-505-2 ebook: 978-1-78099-018-7

Punk Science
Inside the Mind of God
Manjir Samanta-Laughton
Many have experienced unexplainable phenomena; God, psychic
abilities, extraordinary healing and angelic encounters. Can
cutting-edge science actually explain phenomena
previously thought of as 'paranormal'?
Paperback: 978-1-90504-793-2

The Vagabond Spirit of Poetry
Edward Clarke
Spend time with the wisest poets of the modern age and of the
past, and let Edward Clarke remind you of the importance of
poetry in our industrialized world.
Paperback: 978-1-78279-370-0 ebook: 978-1-78279-369-4

Readers of ebooks can buy or view any of these bestsellers by
clicking on the live link in the title. Most titles are published in
paperback and as an ebook. Paperbacks are available in traditional
bookshops. Both print and ebook formats are available online.
Find more titles and sign up to our readers' newsletter at
http://www.johnhuntpublishing.com/non-fiction
Follow us on Facebook at
https://www.facebook.com/JHPNonFiction
and Twitter at https://twitter.com/JHPNonFiction